Best of Alberta
OUTDOOR ACTIVITIES
IN ALBERTA'S HEARTLAND

Best of Alberta
OUTDOOR ACTIVITIES
IN ALBERTA'S HEARTLAND

Whitecap Books / *Vancouver* / *Toronto*

Edited by Linda Ostrowalker
Cover and interior design by Carolyn Deby
Cover photograph by Steve Short/First Light
Interior photographs by Bill Corbett
Typeset by CompuType, Vancouver, B.C.
Printed and bound in Canada by
    D.W. Friesen and Sons Ltd., Altona, Manitoba

Canadian Cataloguing in Publication Data
    Corbett, Bill.
    Outdoor activities in Alberta's heartland
    (The Best of Alberta)

    Includes bibliographical references and index.
    ISBN 1-55110-064-9
    1. Outdoor recreation—Alberta—Guidebooks.
    2. Alberta—Guidebooks. I. Title. II. Series
FC3657.C67 1993   917.12304'3   C93-091148-2
F1076.C67 1993

Table of Contents

Preface

*I*n an age of cross training and triathlons, perhaps a book like this was inevitable. Where once people might have focused on summer hiking, they now also dabble in mountain biking and canoeing. This book is for them and everyone else who wants a diversified taste of all that southern and western Alberta has to offer.

While many people pursue a number of outdoor activities, others are content, or able, to tackle just a few trips a year or season. In either case, they often don't have time to see or do as much as they'd like in the outdoors. When they do go on a hike or bike ride, they often want to make the most of their precious time by embarking on one of the so-called classics. Yet they are confronted in some cases with dozens if not hundreds of options.

The same scenario awaits the visitor who in a few days or weeks wishes to sample Alberta's best landscapes. Several times I have encountered foreigners who, having completed one backpack, wanted to know what other overnight trips they could attempt. Many others plan, while visiting a particular area, to do a couple of hikes, a representative mountain bike trip, and perhaps a quick river outing.

This, then, is an attempt to offer the best trips southern and western Alberta has to offer in six outdoor activities— hiking, backpacking, canoeing, mountain biking, road cycling, and back country skiing.

Choosing the Trips

Attempting to choose a relative handful of the best trips from an area as vast and diversified as southern Alberta is an open invitation to second guessing. Undoubtedly, many readers will think their favourite outings have been overlooked, although some will secretly be glad if their favourite haunts are not exposed. Others will disagree vehemently with the selections for a variety of reasons.

Even trips that draw unanimous rave reviews can prove a miserable experience if you're slogging through mud or lost in a fog. This is especially true of alpine trips such as the Skyline Trail or the Wapta Traverse, either of which can be the best or worst trip in the world based solely on the weather.

Admittedly, this is a highly subjective exercise. When compiling this list, I consulted a number of active outdoors people and pored over specialized guidebooks and trip reports. But ultimately I chose trips that most appealed to me at the time. In five years, my selections might be quite different.

If I have a bias, it is in favour of trips that lead to alpine environments and other places that offer extensive views. I have selected a number of trips enclosed primarily in forests, which certainly have much to recommend them. But if you're wondering why so many trips seem to ascend to high places, you have been forewarned.

Geography

One of the virtues of a diversified guidebook like this is it, by necessity, forces one to visit a wide variety of landscapes and locations in southern and western Alberta. The terrain covered in this book embraces not only the mountain parks of Banff, Jasper, Waterton, and Kananaskis Country but also extends through the foothills and well onto the prairie. Indeed, some of the best canoe trips wind slowly through the prairie region. Similarly, some of the most interesting road cycling trips loop through farm and ranch lands that ordinarily would not be considered tourist country. Those seeking the best mountain biking terrain are compelled to visit the neglected foothills and ridges of Kananaskis Country.

Nonetheless, a solid majority of the trips are located in the mountainous regions of Alberta. There are several reasons for this. First, the mountains, and their flora and fauna, are almost entirely protected within national or provincial parks. Second, they contain many established and well-maintained trails. Third, they are, as public lands, open to all visitors and in most cases easily accessed by good highways. Fourth, frankly it's hard to beat the stunning and varied scenery Alberta's mountain parks have to offer. Millions of tourists who flock to these parks each year can't be wrong, though many have yet to discover the magnificence of a latecomer, Kananaskis Country.

A note to those wondering why splendid destinations such as Lake O'Hara, Mount Robson, Assiniboine, Yoho Valley, and the Kootenays have apparently been overlooked. The reason is simple: this book is intended to cover trips in Alberta, although a couple do stray briefly into British Columbia.

For Nora and John,
who sparked an interest

Acknowledgements

*R*esearching and writing an eclectic book such as this would not have been possible without the assistance of many people. While I have travelled all but a couple of the routes described in this book, it was often in the company of other hikers, skiers, backpackers, canoeists, and cyclists. Some friends let me peer into their journals and secret black books of favourite trips, while others lent gear, provided accommodation, and offered their expertise and moral support.

These contributors include Teresa Michalak, Forbes and Cameron Macdonald, Bob Sharpe, Nancy and Dennis Stefani, Anders Renborg, Greg Zinter, Roman Pachovsky, Guy McLaughlin, Mary Corbett and Graeme Dales, Paula Beauchamp, Vivian Allard, Helen Corbett, and Susanne Swibold. I would also like to thank the staff of the Canadian Parks Service and Kananaskis Country for their assistance, and Linda Ostrowalker for her sensitive editing. Over the past dozen years, I have done many of these trips (in some cases a number of times) in the company of other people too numerous to mention. Their silent contribution is also acknowledged.

Lower Headwall Lake.

Introduction

How to Use this Guide

*E*ach chapter in this guidebook covers a different discipline. In order of appearance, they are hiking, backpacking, canoeing, mountain biking, road cycling, and back country skiing. At the beginning of each chapter is an introduction that covers the type of trips described as well as such things as ethics, ratings, and a check-list of equipment needed for that discipline. In all cases, a rudimentary knowledge of the activity is assumed.

The trips in each chapter are listed in order of increasing difficulty and are thus not grouped geographically. Anyone wishing to do several trips, perhaps involving more than one discipline, while in a specific area, such as Lake Louise, should consult the geographical cross-referencing of trips at the back of this book. At the beginning of each trip description is a list of important information designed to help readers quickly gauge the suitability of a trip for their abilities and desires. This information is listed under the following headings:

Rating: Each trip is given a rating, generally covering three levels of difficulty: moderate, intermediate, and advanced.

The type of ratings used change somewhat according to the activity. Canoeing, for example, uses a universally recognized system based on paddling proficiency and rapids encountered. See the introduction of each chapter for an explanation of how the ratings apply to specific activities.

Distance: In almost all cases, this refers to the distance, in kilometres, of a trip from start to finish, whether it's one way, a loop, or a return along the same route as the approach. It does not refer to the distance travelled by road to return to the trailhead in cases where the start and finish are at different locations. The distance listed also refers to the major destination of the trip and does not include side-trips mentioned along the way.

Time: I once asked a seasoned mountaineer how long it took to complete a particular trip. He replied he never kept track of time while in the mountains. A laudable approach, to be sure, but those reading trip descriptions still like a rough idea of whether they'll be out by lunch or groping back by headlamp. The emphasis here is on the word rough. What a fit and single-minded person might tackle in two hours might take the uninitiated or the wanderer five or six. I have tried to estimate how much time the average person would need to complete these trips, knowing some people will take longer and others less. These times give some allowance for rest stops, lunches, picture taking, and gazing but do not include side-trips, long naps in meadows, or prolonged rambles.

Elevation Gained: This refers to the difference in elevation from the start of the trip to the high point along the way. It does not include the total amount of elevation gained along the way, which would be impossible to gauge, given the ups and downs of most trails. Elevation gain gives readers a rough idea of how much uphill exertion is required on a trip. As a general rule, a relatively fit adult hiker will take a little more than thirty minutes to gain 300 metres (1000 feet) in elevation. Obviously, a backpacker will take somewhat longer. Generally, a gain of less than 300 metres is considered moderate, more than 900 metres very strenuous. Elevation gain is not listed for essentially level cycling trips and obviously not mentioned at all for canoe trips.

Maps: For hiking, backpacking, mountain biking, and back country skiing, the relevant National Topographical System (NTS) 1:50,000 maps are listed. Note: Not all trails are shown on these maps and in some cases trail routes have changed since the maps were published. For canoe trips, the maps listed are 1:50,000 and, in some cases, 1:250,000 NTS maps. Road cyclists can use Alberta highway maps or a similar Alberta cyclists' map that shows traffic densities and shoulder widths for specific stretches of Alberta highways. Maps are generally available at map stores, specialty outdoor shops, Maps Alberta (usually Alberta Forestry Lands & Wildlife offices), and federal Maps & Surveys in Edmonton and the Geological Survey of Canada in Calgary. Hint: To gain an overview of areas you plan to travel in, it's worth buying the 1:200,000 maps published by the Canadian Parks Service. These maps cover large areas such as the entirety of Jasper National Park and of Banff, Yoho, and Kootenay national parks.

Access: This provides information on how to get to the start of a trip, usually from the nearest major highway. For example, the access for most Kananaskis Country trips is described from the Trans-Canada Highway 40 junction west of Calgary. This also describes where to leave pick-up vehicles, or bicycles, when the trip ends at a different location than its start.

The actual route descriptions are fairly straightforward. Generally, the first paragraph highlights why I consider this to be one of the best trips of its kind in western and southern Alberta. This allows readers to quickly decide if they are interested in a given trip. Although the format changes somewhat from trip to trip, the second and sometimes third paragraphs usually outline what may be involved in embarking on a trip and when it is best attempted.

The route descriptions are intended as a general guide of how to get from start to finish, without being so detailed as to remove the surprise of discovery. These trip descriptions are somewhat longer than those found in most guidebooks, the aim being to inject a bit of history, geology, wildlife, plant life, or just personal experience into the proceedings.

Important Information

Weather

The only certainty about Alberta's weather is its unpredictability. Winter temperatures in southern Alberta have been known to rise by more than thirty degrees Celsius in the space of a few hours when a chinook blows in. Similarly, clear blue skies can quickly give way to thunderstorms, a particular concern when stuck out in the open or the rain jacket has been left in the car.

In the mountains, the weather is even more subject to sudden change. Mountain forecasts are particularly unreliable, tending to cover large areas and ignoring the isolated weather patterns common in the mountains. They should thus be treated as general guidelines rather than gospel. As a rule, I don't pay much attention to these forecasts until a day or two before embarking on a trip. Having said that, it is often sunny in the mountains while raining in the city or clear over the patch of mountains you are travelling through. Sometimes, as the saying goes, you just have to go out there and rub your nose in it. The best advice, whenever you head out, is to be prepared for anything.

Generally, the southern half of Alberta is, by Canadian standards, blessed with a fairly moderate climate. Temperatures typically reach into the twenties in summer and hover below freezing in winter, with occasional periods dipping below minus thirty degrees Celsius. Mind you, Calgary, for instance, has had snowstorms in August and weeks on end of above freezing temperatures in winter.

Looking south to Mount Balfour and its north glacier.

Alberta's Rocky Mountains, rising in places to nearly 3500 metres, often create their own weather. The higher peaks have a polar climate, where snow is present year-round in the form of glaciers. While wetter than the rest of the province, snowfall in the Rockies is both lighter and drier than in the interior ranges of British Columbia. Overall precipitation levels in southern Alberta are moderate, approaching desertlike conditions in the south and east.

The winds, however, are above average in intensity. The further south one goes, the stronger they get, particularly through passes like the Crowsnest in southwestern Alberta. Of the major areas described in this book, Waterton is easily the windiest, followed by Kananaskis Country. In winter, strong, warm chinook winds often flow over the eastern slopes of the Rockies and onto the plains. Chinooks, named after an Indian tribe living in the Columbia River basin, are preceded by a tell-tale arch of clouds and, for some people, by migraine headaches.

Wildlife

In Alberta, one can find everything from the tiny pygmy

shrew to the wood bison, the largest mammal in North America. Common large mammals include elk, moose, mule and white-tailed deer, bighorn sheep, mountain goats, and, in the far south, pronghorn antelope. Carnivores include wolves, wolverines, cougars, and coyotes, but you're unlikely to see any of these predators standing in your path.

In the air and on the water, one can find numerous songbirds, migratory waterfowl, eagles, hawks, crows, ravens, hummingbirds, herons, swallows, and dippers, to name a few. In the alpine zone, ptarmigan can be found year-round.

Of course, what many an outdoorsperson wants to know is what critters can kill, maim, or wound him? Rattlesnakes, black widow spiders, and even scorpions can be found in the desertlike environment of eastern and southern Alberta, particularly on canoe trips through the prairies. There have been rare reports of coyotes biting campers, though they're more likely to take off with a cat or small dog. A moose in rut is an animal to definitely avoid. Surprisingly, some elk have shed their mild-mannered traits and become more aggressive. In recent years, there have been increasing instances of female elk attacking pedestrians who venture too near their young in the middle of Banff townsite. Invariably, the odd person catches an accidental swing of the antlers when they edge too close for a full-frame photo.

The best course of action is to keep a respectful distance. Remember, these are wild animals and somewhat unpredictable, though not nearly as much so as humans. In most places, it is against the law to feed wildlife. This philosophy should also be applied to feeding professional beggars like gray jays (whiskey jacks) and ground squirrels.

Bears

The average visitor to the mountains is far more likely to be involved in a car accident, fall victim to hypothermia, or be caught in an avalanche than attacked by a black or grizzly bear. Yet because bears, particularly grizzlies, have the ability to kill or maul and are somewhat unpredictable, there is a fear of their presence out of proportion to their potential threat.

Consider that grizzly bears in Alberta's mountain parks number in the hundreds, compared with the millions of people that pass through the parks and the scores that venture out of their cars. Confrontations are generally rare, although some years (such as when the berry crop is poor) there seem to be a spate of attacks and the odd death. The increased use of mountain bikes, which move quickly and quietly, could result in more confrontations.

Fortunately, more people are becoming aware of what to do and not do to avoid bear confrontations and attacks. Generally, common sense and awareness are the best preventive measures. Remember, you are a guest in their territory. For detailed information, read *Bear Attacks—Their Causes and Avoidance,* by Stephen Herrero (1985. Nick Lyons Books). Here, as a general review, are some of the more salient points to avoiding bear confrontations.

- When camping in every season but winter, always put your food up a bear pole or at least suspend it high in a tree well removed from your tent. Never keep in your tent any food or other smelly items, including toothpaste.
- Make lots of noise while in bear country, especially when travelling in heavily wooded areas and near streams. When the wind is blowing towards you, it is especially important to make noise when approaching blind corners or cresting hills. What to make noise with? A bear bell is not only apt to annoy your companions seeking the quiet of the woods but is also questionably effective. You're just as well off, if not better, to make periodic shouting or whooping sounds. This task can be alternated between group members or shared as an a cappella arrangement.
- Bear bells have increasingly been replaced by bear

repellents as a line of defence. These high-powered sprays eject a dose of capsaicin, an active ingredient in cayenne pepper, toward the bear's eyes and snout, hopefully scaring it away while doing no permanent damage. While it may be difficult to effectively use such sprays in an emergency, they provide peace of mind for many people.

- When confronted by a bear, the best strategy is to either quietly back away or, if attack seems imminent, to play dead. This latter strategy has often proved effective in cases where bears—particularly mothers with cubs—have been startled. In situations where the bear seems intent on eating a victim—such as when dragging someone from a tent—fighting off the attack may be the only salvation.

Water

I have for years dipped water bottles and cups into alpine streams with no ill effects. But maybe I've just been lucky. Officials in the mountain parks are increasingly recommending against such practices because untreated water may contain *Giardia lamblia*. This is a parasite carried in the feces of humans and other animals that can wreak havoc on the intestinal system. The best prevention is to boil drinking, cooking, and washing water for five minutes or put it through a portable ceramic filter. Iodine and other chemical treatments will often not kill the parasite.

First Aid

If you spend much time in the outdoors, you should consider enrolling in a first aid course dedicated to outdoor or wilderness pursuits. As well as covering the basics, such as cardiopulmonary resuscitation, these courses deal with outdoor-related problems such as hypothermia, treating avalanche victims, and dealing with injuries and illnesses far from help.

Here is a short check-list of what to put in a first aid kit. It can be expanded or contracted as needed. There should be at least one first aid kit per party.

- Pocket- or pamphlet-sized first aid manual
- Several triangular bandages—Large pieces of cotton, folded and used for binding wounds, immobilizing injured areas, or tying splints. A bandanna, t-shirt, or other apparel can be used in a pinch.
- Bandages—A selection of one-inch and butterfly bandages
- Sterile gauze pads for larger wounds
- Carlisle "Battle" dressing or a sanitary napkin for heavy bleeding
- Antiseptic ointment or towelettes
- Tensor bandage for wrapping sprains or sore knees
- Adhesive tape—A length wrapped around a film canister can save weight
- Painkillers
- Moleskin for blisters
- Safety pins
- Two quarters for phone calls

Everything will fit into a small rigid plastic container or a heavy-duty freezer bag. Additional items, more for repairs or emergencies, should include a pocket knife (preferably with tweezers and scissors), a butane lighter or waterproof matches, a short pencil, a small sewing kit, and a small tube of all-purpose glue. A pocket-sized space blanket weighs only ounces and can retain body heat in an emergency. After experiencing one shivering bivouac on an exposed mountainside, I always carry one.

Regulations

All back country campers in Alberta's national parks must obtain a park use permit. They are available without charge

Cycling through Little Elbow Pass with Misty Range peaks in the background.

at information centres and some warden offices in the respective parks or through the Canadian Parks Service regional office in Calgary (see **Useful Contact Numbers** below). Back country campsite bookings can be made up to twenty-one days in advance. Such permits are not required in Kananaskis Country, although back country campers can register their trips at visitor information centres or at some trailheads.

In the national parks, back country users can voluntarily register their trips at warden offices. This is recommended for longer and more difficult outings. These registrations provide wardens with trip particulars so rescues can be mounted if the party does not return on time. Currently, there is no charge for such rescues when warranted. Just make sure you sign back in or phone upon returning.

Valid fishing licences are required for angling in the national parks. They are available at park information centres and area sporting goods stores. An Alberta licence is required for fishing outside the national parks.

Back Country Ethics

When you venture into the outdoors, consider yourself a privileged guest. Respecting both parks and private lands will help ensure their long-term preservation.

* Practice minimal-impact camping techniques. Camp and build fires in designated areas or, where allowed, in areas that will suffer the least amount of environmental damage.
* Pack out all garbage.
* Do not remove wild flowers, plants, trees, fossils, or rocks. In most parks, it is illegal.
* Keep a respectful distance from all wildlife and do not feed wild animals or birds.
* Stay on established trails. Do not take short cuts, especially on switchbacks, as they can lead to further erosion.

Useful Contact Numbers

All phone number area codes are 403.

Canadian Parks Service – Western Regional Office (covers all Alberta mountain national parks) – Information 292-4401. Back country conditions 292-6600. 220-4 Avenue S.E., Calgary, Alberta T2P 3H8

Kananaskis Country – Main office – 297-3362. Suite 100, 1011 Glenmore Trail S.W., Calgary, Alberta T2V 4R6

Banff Information Centre – 762-1550

Banff Warden Office – 762-4506

Banff Weather (Environment Canada) – 762-2088

Lake Louise Warden Office – 522-3866

Jasper Information Centre – 852-6786

Jasper Warden Office – 852-6156

Jasper Weather (Environment Canada) – 852-3185

Waterton Warden Office – 859-2477

Waterton Park Information – 859-5105

Peter Lougheed Provincial Park – 591-7222

Travel Alberta – 1-800-222-6501

Avalanche Information (Alberta and B.C.) –
1-800-667-1105

Hostelling International – Calgary office – 283-5551;
Edmonton office – 432-7798

Alpine Club of Canada (hut bookings) – Main office,
Canmore – 678-3200

Alberta River Forecast Centre – River flows from May to
October – 1-800-661-8917

Hiker standing above hole in rock on Mount Tyrwhitt.

CHAPTER ONE

Hikes

Introduction

*A*lberta's Rockies offer some of the finest mountain scenery in the world. While most people view it from the highway, the best way to experience the subalpine forests, alpine meadows, and lakes is on foot.

Hikers in the Canadian Rockies enjoy the best of two worlds. Much of our mountain terrain is protected within national and provincial parks. At the same time, these areas have been explored on foot for many years. As a result, there is an excellent system of trails throughout the mountains, ranging from groomed interpretive walks to well-beaten paths into wilderness areas. Nearly all of these trails are accessible from major highways.

Still, there is rarely the feeling of being crowded. Despite the millions of people who pass along these highways each year, a fifteen-minute walk beyond the trailhead usually leaves civilization far behind. Indeed, an early start on most of the trails described in this chapter will likely result in few human encounters, at least on the way in. It's somewhat surprising these trails are not more crowded, given the international fame of Alberta's mountain national parks—Banff, Jasper, and Waterton—and the rising stature of Kananaskis Country.

Ratings

Certainly, one can find crowds of pedestrians in our mountain parks but not in the destinations described in this book. With one or two exceptions, these outings steer clear of the highly popular and the paved, the tourist strolls, and the interpretive walks, which are well covered in the tourist literature. Instead, these outings go into the back country, to reveal Alberta's magnificent mountain scenery at its uncrowded best.

Many of these trips pass through a number of climatic zones en route to alpine terrain. As a result, they usually gain a considerable amount of elevation. Those embarking on most of these trips should be reasonably fit and willing to invest some exertion for the reward of alpine views.

Moderate: A trip of one or two hours with less than 300 metres of elevation gain.

Moderate to Strenuous: A good half-day's outing with an elevation gain of more than 300 metres and a distance of less than 10 kilometres return.

Strenuous: With a few exceptions, a full day's outing, involving an elevation gain of more than 450 metres and a distance of between 10 and 15 kilometres return. The exceptions cover shorter distances but require steeper ascents.

Strenuous to Advanced: A full day's outing, often no longer than strenuous trips, but requiring an elevation gain of more than 650 metres. These trips may involve a bit of scrambling, some exposure to drop-offs, and steeper descents over scree.

Advanced: A full day's outing with significant elevation gain and some of the elements described in **Strenuous to Advanced.** The added difficulty is the lack of trail in places, requiring some route finding.

Hiking Check-list

Fortunately, you don't need a lot of equipment to enjoy hiking. A good pair of hiking shoes, some clothing, and water can take you a long ways in the mountains.

Having said that, one should never venture into the mountains unprepared. Though the trip may be short and the day sunny, mountain weather can quickly and unexpectedly turn nasty. Ventures into the alpine can also expose hikers to high winds. Remember, hypothermia can set in even on sunny summer days. And if you twist an ankle, the wonderful solitude of the mountains now means you might be stranded many kilometres from help.

The moral is: Carry enough clothing and emergency supplies to deal with the unexpected. You'll soon get used to the few extra kilograms that can save a life in the mountains.

- Footwear—Sturdy, lightweight hiking shoes or boots with mountaineering or equivalent soles
- Two pairs of socks—Wool, polypropylene (it's come a long ways), or a blend of the two. Some socks are reinforced under the heels and balls of the feet. Carry a spare pair in case your feet get wet.
- Shorts—Stretchy or nylon
- Walking pants—Synthetic quick-dry pants are fairly windproof, breathable, and resist a certain amount of moisture. Avoid cotton, which is cold when wet.
- Rain pants and jacket or the more expensive waterproof-breathable outfits, preferably with full-length zippers for ease of putting on and venting. A coated nylon poncho will do in a pinch.
- T-shirt, preferably long sleeved (remember, suntans are now a bad thing). A white, long-sleeved polypropylene top is thin, reflects the sun, and dries quickly. Again, avoid cotton.
- Light wool sweater or pile/fleece jacket with full zipper
- Thin pair of gloves

- Broad-brimmed hat
- Good sunglasses
- Sun cream with at least an SPF rating of 15
- Bandanna—Protects the neck and can double as a cool face-cloth
- One-litre water bottle per person
- First aid kit—At least one per party
- Moleskin for blisters
- Pocket knife
- Pocket-sized emergency space blanket
- Energy bar, in addition to lunch
- Safety pin—Use to pin your car keys to inside pack pocket. Also serves to reattach broken pack straps.
- Bear repellent (optional)
- Insect repellent
- Camera and sufficient film
- Topo map—Even if you don't get lost, a map helps identify nearby peaks and drainages
- Green plastic garbage bag—Covers pack in a down-pour, or you in an emergency

BEAR'S HUMP

• **Rating:** Moderate • **Distance:** 2.4 kilometres return • **Time:** 1–2 hours • **Elevation Gain:** 215 metres (700 feet) • **Topo Map:** Waterton Lakes National Park • **Access:** The trail departs into the woods from the rear of the Waterton Lakes National Park information centre near the entrance to Waterton townsite.

DESPITE ITS BREVITY, the Bear's Hump trail leads to one of the most marvellous viewpoints in the Canadian Rockies. From this lofty perch, hikers look over the town of Waterton and down the length of Upper Waterton Lake into the United States. At the same time, they can turn slightly

Overlooking Upper Waterton Lake from the Bear's Hump.

left and suddenly the endless vista of mountains is replaced by an expanse of Alberta prairie.

This is no interpretive stroll. You probably never thought a 1-kilometre hike could take so long or climb so high—more than 200 metres. Still, many children and seniors make it to the top, with the odd stop along the way. For those who would not normally venture past a roadside viewpoint, this is an excellent chance to see what attracts eagles and mountaineers to the rocky heights. It's also a short enough trip for imaginative hikers to pack a back country stove, cook supper on top, and watch the sun go down.

The term Bear's Hump refers to Mount Crandell's former name of Black Bear Mountain; the hump is at the far end of a ridge descending south from Crandell. The limestone and dolomite cliffs of Bear's Hump were at one time attached to a rock wall extending across the valley to Vimy Peak. The wall was worn away by an advancing glacier, which scoured a 150-metre-deep basin that now contains Upper Waterton Lake, the deepest lake in the Canadian Rockies. From the elevated Bear's Hump, the effects of this glaciation are clearly visible in the U-shaped valley to the south.

The trail winds up the forested south ridge of Mount Crandell. The path is broad and smooth, the many switchbacking corners near the top secured with boards. As you climb through a forest of aspen, fir, and pine, watch for deer, which are frequently seen throughout the lower woodlands of Waterton Lakes National Park.

Suddenly the trail breaks through the forest to an exposed, rocky ledge—the Bear's Hump. Be careful not to stray too close to the edge, which is slippery when wet, or throw rocks, as climbers may be scaling the cliffs below. Just look below to the town of Waterton, which extends on an alluvial fan into the narrow neck of water separating Upper and Middle Waterton lakes. On this side of the strait, the historic Prince of Wales Hotel sits on a small hill that offers expansive views down the upper lake.

Your economy view, however, is much grander, extending far south over Upper Waterton Lake and its flanking rows of peaks to the U.S. Glacier National Park. In 1932, Waterton-Glacier International Peace Park was created, partly in recognition of the upper lake's straddling of the U.S.-Canada border. Though the two parks retain distinct identities, their administrators work together on such things as wildlife management and ecosystem conservation.

This viewpoint also provides graphic evidence of how the mountains of Waterton rise almost straight out of the prairies to the north without a foothills transition zone. The dramatic contrast is the result of the mountain building process here, in which huge blocks of sedimentary rocks, more than a billion years old, moved east and were thrust over top of younger rocks.

If this short hike has whetted your appetite for further adventure, you can continue scrambling for awhile up the south ridge of Mount Crandell. While doing so, scan the terrain above for much more adroit scramblers, bighorn sheep.

Return the same way, taking care not to take short cuts on the switchbacks, thus saving the hillside from unnecessary erosion.

CAVELL MEADOWS-ANGEL GLACIER LOOP

• **Rating:** Moderately Strenuous • **Distance:** 8 kilometres return • **Time:** 3–4 hours • **Elevation Gain:** 400 metres (1300 feet) • **Topo Map:** 83 D/9 Amethyst Lakes • **Access:** Drive 7.5 kilometres south of Jasper townsite on Highway 93 (Icefields Parkway) and take 93A, to the right, for 5 kilometres to the Edith Cavell junction. Turn right and follow the switchbacking road for 14.2 kilometres to its terminus below the north face of Mount Edith Cavell. The trailhead is at the far end of the parking lot.

THIS CIVILIZED ROUTE beneath the looming north face of Mount Edith Cavell is one of the best short hikes in the Rockies. Where else can one walk along a glacial moraine, gaze up at ice avalanches cascading off a 1400-metre wall, and wander through a flower-filled alpine meadow, all in the space of three kilometres? This trip also offers hikers a good education in the surprisingly recent effects of glaciation in the Rockies.

The trail to Cavell Meadows is a steady climb that gains some 400 metres over 3 kilometres. But the trail is excellent throughout with strategically placed benches along the lower, paved sections. In any event, this hike naturally encourages a leisurely pace and many stops along the way. It's best attempted during the brief weeks of midsummer when the snows have departed and the alpine flowers are in full bloom. Unless you get an early morning start, expect lots of company on this popular walk, especially over the first kilometre.

Above the parking lot, one is immediately confronted by the powerful forces of glaciation. The rock rim you are standing on is part of a terminal moraine left by a glacial advance

Angel Glacier from the Cavell Meadows trail.

that peaked around the turn of this century. Note the rocky ridges, known as lateral moraines, deposited by the glacier along both sides of the valley. A subsequent warming trend has caused the glacier to beat a hasty retreat. The remnant Angel Glacier has retracted its tongue up the steep wall of Edith Cavell toward its glacial cirque, where the blue ice is still firmly entrenched. Above the glacier, the magnificent north face of Edith Cavell continues to rise, its quartzite cliffs retaining horizontal bands of snow well into the summer. A number of expert climbers have scaled this big wall, generally choosing routes less exposed to the dangerous ice and rock fall that daily entertains tourists. Frequently, climbers can be seen ascending the drier and safer rock routes above the parking lot.

In the early 1800s, the mountain was called Montagne de la Grande Traverse by passing fur brigades on their way over the Rockies. It was renamed Edith Cavell for a British nurse executed by the Germans for helping Allied prisoners escape from Brussels during World War I. At 3363 metres (11,033 feet), it is the highest and most recognized peak near Jasper.

From the parking lot, hikers follow the paved trail alongside the jumbled boulders of the near lateral moraine. These lichen-covered quartz rocks harbour two year-round residents, the tiny, tailless pika and the shaggy-coated marmot. Both are usually heard before seen, the marmot emitting a whistling sound, the pika a high-pitched squeak.

At pavement's end, take the left trail, which switchbacks up and then alongside the moraine before disappearing into thick stands of fir and spruce. Soon the forest gives way to a meadow ablaze in midsummer with Indian paintbrush, heather, and fleabane. A viewpoint provides a bird's-eye look across to the Angel Glacier, its extended "wings" clearly visible from this height.

The trail continues to loop up through the meadow. Though the open terrain and the ridge beyond are enticing, stay on the path to help protect this fragile environment.

The trail now begins to descend, re-entering the forest and then rejoining the main trail at a lower viewpoint.

Once back at the junction, follow the crowds left along the Path of the Glacier trail as it swings back through the glacier-scoured valley. This trail descends to a small body of blue meltwater, which supports a flotilla of white ice chunks severed from the glacier above. Below the lake, the path makes its way through boulders and gravelly flats. As recently as the 1950s, glacier ice extended down this valley. Today, willows and spruce are reclaiming the rocky ground. Follow the trail back to the parking lot.

WILCOX PASS

• **Rating:** Moderately Strenuous • **Distance:** 8 kilometres return • **Time:** About 4 hours • **Elevation Gain:** 335 metres (1100 feet) • **Topo Maps:** 83 C/3 Columbia Icefield and 83 C/6 Sunwapta Peak • **Access:** The trailhead is located at the start of the road leading into the Wilcox Campground, 2.8 kilometres south of the Columbia Icefield Information Centre or 2 kilometres north of the Banff-Jasper boundary.

OVERSHADOWED BY THE icy charms of Athabasca Glacier across the road, the alpine meadow rising to Wilcox Pass is one of the neglected jewels of the Rockies. The lofty view of Mount Athabasca and the edge of the Columbia Icefield are more dazzling than from the crowded parking lot below. But the rolling terrain that stretches to the horizon and the bighorn sheep that haunt its slopes are reasons enough to take this short, steep hike.

For the first kilometre, the well-beaten trail rises softly through a mature stand of Engelmann spruce and alpine fir. The forest is soon replaced by an open hillside of stunted trees, willows, and, higher, wild flowers.

This open hillside offers a bird's-eye look across at four 3350-metre (11,000-foot) peaks—the gleaming white

Athabasca, the attached Andromeda and, to the right of the Athabasca Glacier, Snow Dome and Kitchener. Far below, giant snowcoaches look like toys as they haul tourists up the lower glacier, which descends in a tongue from the level vastness of the Columbia Icefield, Canada's largest. Those equipped with binoculars might spot climbers ascending Athabasca, perhaps the most popular summit in Canada. By contrast, Snow Dome looks uninspiring. Yet it is the hydrological apex of North America, its melting snows and ice feeding rivers that eventually flow into three oceans.

Closer at hand, bighorn sheep can often be seen grazing on the slopes below Wilcox Pass. While bighorns are a common sight along the highway and sometimes a begging nuisance, a glimpse of a wild ram lifting its curved rack to eye an intruder is a magical sight. This is also excellent terrain for spotting another large mammal you won't want to encounter at close quarters, the grizzly bear.

The pass was named for U.S. mountaineer and explorer, Walter Wilcox, one of several climbers seeking two mythical 5000-metre peaks, Hooker and Brown, which turned out to be some 2000 metres lower. When Wilcox came up the Athabasca Valley in 1896, glacial ice filled the valley where the highway now runs. He and others used this route as an alternative to the narrow Athabasca Valley which, north of the Athabasca Glacier, was choked with debris from a rock slide.

A steep section of trail above a narrow gulley is soon forgotten as the rolling meadow opens up to reveal the rising ridge of Mount Wilcox. At 4 kilometres, one reaches the height of the pass, which is marked by a large cairn and a rusted sign. It is somewhat surprising at such elevation to discover two sizable marshy ponds thick with reeds and yellow algae scum.

While one is tempted to rest here and enjoy the scenery, it's worth walking through the long, open meadows beyond or scrambling up the nearby ridge of Mount Wilcox for an even more encompassing view of the Icefield. Stay on the trail wherever possible to help preserve this delicate landscape.

Hikers looking for an additional challenge can hike another 7 kilometres beyond the pass to Tangled Falls and the intersecting Icefield Parkway. From the pass, either stay in the valley bottom or follow a higher series of cairns to the left across a rock slide before descending into the forest below. It's 10 kilometres along the highway back to the trailhead.

In summer, there are regularly scheduled walks to Wilcox Pass with a naturalist.

MOUNT INDEFATIGABLE

• **Rating:** Strenuous • **Distance:** 7.5 kilometres return • **Time:** 3–4 hours • **Elevation Gained:** 500 metres (1640 feet) • **Topo Map:** 82 J/11 Kananaskis Lakes • **Access:** From the Trans-Canada Highway interchange, drive 50 kilometres south on Highway 40, turn right, and follow the Kananaskis Lakes Trail for 15.5 kilometres to the trailhead at the North Interlakes parking lot.

THIS EXCEPTIONAL HIKE provides a rare opportunity to rapidly gain a commanding view over the Kananaskis Valley. Within forty-five minutes of leaving the car, industrious hikers can be standing high on a ridge, looking down on two lakes and across a sea of peaks. The view, however, is hard-earned. The trail takes a beeline up Indefatigable's southeast edge, rising more than 400 metres in the first 3 kilometres.

Indefatigable makes for a good outing in early June, when the snows have departed this exposed escarpment, making room for the blossoming of mostly yellow wild flowers. This is also a good trip for impressing visiting friends or relatives who have time for only one hike in the Rockies. Just make sure their calves are in good shape and their feet tied into

Upper and Lower Kananaskis lakes from Mount Indefatigable trail.

hiking shoes with good traction for the descent over pea gravel.

As an appetizer for the views ahead, the trail begins by following a narrow passageway between the Upper and Lower Kananaskis lakes, with an impressive panorama across the former to Mounts Lyautey and Sarrail. Actually, you are standing on an earth dam, part of a series of hydroelectric developments that have irretrievably changed the Upper and Lower Kananaskis lakes. While the lakes are not without their charms, they apparently pale beside their previous incarnations, when a smaller upper lake was dotted with islands and connected to the lower by a waterfall.

After crossing over a dam gate, follow the north shore trail of Upper Kananaskis Lake very briefly. Take a trail to the right that leads pleasantly up through a cool, mature forest of pine and spruce. The soft path here is littered with orange needles and lined with mosses and early season evergreen violets.

The cool forest is in sharp contrast to the rocky trail ahead, which rises steeply over crumbly rock. In late spring, the lush valley to the left is covered in yellow glacier lilies that mark the departure of the snow cover. On the dry trail, the only running water is down your brow as you scramble on aching calves up to a viewpoint.

A well-placed bench allows you to catch your breath and marvel at the views south across Upper Kananaskis Lake to the walls of glaciated Sarrail, Foch, and Fox. Many of the peaks in this range were named in honour of World War I heroes and tragedies. The peaks across the lake—Foch, Sarrail, Lyautey—bear the names of French generals. The line of Indefatigable, Invincible, Warspite, and Black Prince to the northwest commemorates British battleships and cruisers involved in the Battle of Jutland; all but Warspite went down, with heavy loss of life.

The trail takes a somewhat easier angle as it carries along the edge of this green escarpment. The distant blue waters of Lower Kananaskis Lake appear to be right beneath one's feet here. Take care not to step too close to the edge of this steep cliff. In late spring, this alpine environment supports a profusion of yellow flowers, including delicate inverted glacier lilies.

As the trail finally levels off, it opens up views north along the Kananaskis Valley past the end of the lower lake. The jagged grey peaks of the Opal Range across the way are classic examples of the limestone sawtoothed peaks found in the Front Ranges of the Canadian Rockies. The trail now disappears into trees for a short stretch, ending suddenly at a precipitous drop-off.

Those thirsting for additional adventure can backtrack a short distance and follow a faint trail that carries on toward an outlier to the northeast. Head up grassy slopes to gain a right-hand ridge, which is followed easily to the summit, some 300 metres higher than the main trail. From this lofty spot, one may be able to see an old road that led up the north slope of Indefatigable to a short-lived gypsum mine, abandoned in the late 1960s. As an alternative destination, take a more direct line to the west up scree to a summit equipped with a lookout.

Return the same way, taking care on the slippery pea gravel that covers the dusty rocks on steeper sections above the trees.

SADDLEBACK

• **Rating:** Strenuous • **Distance:** 7.2 kilometres return • **Time:** 3–4 hours • **Elevation Gain:** 580 metres (1900 feet) • **Topo Map:** 82 N/8 Lake Louise • **Access:** Drive 4 kilometres west of Lake Louise townsite to Lake Louise and, just before Chateau Lake Louise, park at the west end of public lot B. The trail is just beyond in the trees: turn left.

FAR ABOVE THE awed hordes who troop along the easier walks around Lake Louise, the Saddleback rewards the strong-legged with one of the most splendid alpine meadows in the Canadian Rockies. Here, amongst the delicate flowers and lichen-covered boulders, one is greeted at eye level by an array of famous big peaks. The spectacular north face of Mount Temple, called the Eiger of the Rockies, is worth the sweat alone. The Saddleback also makes a fine destination in late September when the numerous alpine larch trees have turned their deciduous needles to orange.

Be forewarned the Saddleback trail is unrelentingly uphill, rising nearly 600 metres over its relatively short length. The initial stretch disdains switchbacks for a direct ascent through a mature forest of spruce and fir. Ignore all deviating forks and stay on the main course of this meticulously constructed trail.

An open slope cleared by avalanches is a good place to pause and take in the broad, glaciated valley of the Bow River, which is already far below. Easily visible across the valley is another form of tree clearing, the many runs of the Lake Louise ski hill, where several World Cup downhill races have been staged. Further left is the 3394-metre Mount

Hector, named for the surgeon and geologist who explored much of the Rockies as part of the Palliser Expedition in the late 1850s. Some say the summit resembles Snoopy lying atop his dog house! Closer at hand, along the forest's edge, look for several species of alpine lichen, including one that features tiny lettucelike leaves.

The trail continues to climb as it traverses around the northeastern slopes of Fairview Mountain. Ignore a steep short cut that ascends to the right through enclosed forest and save it for the descent.

The main trail offers graphic evidence of the massive forces of gravity in the mountains. The route traverses several avalanche slopes, where sliding snows have cropped young evergreens and carried mature trees like matchsticks to the valley floor. As the trail ascends in switchbacks, the trees are largely replaced by jumbled fields of boulders, which slid long ago from the surrounding heights and are now clad in green lichen.

The starkness of this landscape is contrasted by the tall larch around which the trail winds to reach a high meadow, where buttercups and western anemones flower among the alpine grasses. Here one finally attains the Saddleback, a shallow, bowl-shaped pass that rises gently to Saddle Mountain on the southeast and Fairview Mountain on the northwest. Despite the sparse cover, this terrain is home to a diversity of wildlife such as pika, squirrels, grouse, bluebirds, and rosy finches. The Saddleback was also home in the 1920s and 1930s to a teahouse, one of three built near Lake Louise by the Canadian Pacific Railway as a tourist complement to its Chateau Lake Louise; the other two are still in service.

The most compelling presence is the nearby north face of Mount Temple, which rises 1500 metres from Lake Annette to its glacier-clad summit. Believe it or not, half a dozen routes have been forged up these sheer walls by some of the finest climbers in North America, though the constant dangers of falling ice and rock have claimed several lives. Several thousand more have reached the 3543-metre summit, the third highest in the southern Canadian Rockies, by the much easier southwest ridge, which ascends on the right-hand skyline from Sentinel Pass.

Return the same way, taking the short cut, if you desire. While you're in the area, it's worth taking a short walk around the famous lake. Try to imagine the reaction of packer Tom Wilson in 1882, when he was guided here by a Stoney Indian, thus becoming the first white person to visit this magical spot. Drop into the mammoth Chateau Lake Louise, which dates back to 1890, for a well-deserved afternoon tea.

Fairview Mountain Option

Those with energy to spare can hike another 425 vertical metres (1400 feet) from the Saddleback to the summit of Mount Fairview for an even more spectacular vista. From the cairn at the top of the pass, turn right and follow a well-beaten path that climbs through larch and then switchbacks steeply up the southeast scree slopes of Fairview.

Mount Fairview is apparently named for its good weather when surrounding peaks are swathed in clouds. But on one visit, I was greeted at the top by an early September snowstorm, which of course gave way to blue skies as soon as I descended into the valley.

As is the case with many mountains, the top is farther than it looks. Be prepared for an hour's slog. The views, however, are well worth the effort, encompassing the glaciated Mounts Lefroy and Victoria (both exceeding 3400 metres) and, a vertical kilometre below, the exquisite turquoise waters of Lake Louise. Those equipped with binoculars can likely make out tourists trekking along the lake to teahouses at Agnes Lake and the Plain of Six Glaciers.

Be careful not to stray too close to the edge. A hiker fell

to his death here in the summer of 1992. Return along the path to the Saddleback or, if adventurous, take a more direct line down the scree.

BURSTALL PASS

• **Rating:** Strenuous • **Distance:** 15 kilometres return • **Time:** 5–6 hours • **Elevation Gain:** 460 metres (1500 feet) • **Topo Maps:** 82 J/14 Spray Lakes Reservoir and 82 J/11 Kananaskis Lakes • **Access:** From the junction with Highway 40, drive 22.5 kilometres north on the Smith-Dorrien-Spray Trail to the trailhead at the Mud Lake parking lot. • **Note:** Burstall Pass receives significant amounts of snow, which also makes it a popular early winter destination for intermediate back country skiers.

BURSTALL PASS IS one of the finest and most fascinating day hikes in Kananaskis Country. Getting there is a good part of the fun, as the route passes a sizable glacier, crosses braided streams, and leads up through a long, subalpine

Mount Birdwood and the Burstall Valley from near Burstall Pass.

meadow. But the pass—unlike many rocky, windswept cols—is easily the highlight of this intermediate hike. It features unusual, fractured topography, splendid views, and ample opportunity to ramble for hours through rolling alpine terrain.

Save this trip until mid-July when the heavy snow pack along the continental divide, that marks the pass, has all but disappeared. The walking is fairly level, save for two steeper sections, the last rising to Burstall Pass. The route is well marked to the pass.

From the parking lot, cross an earthen dam over the south end of Mud Lake, which sits on a small divide, its outlet streams flowing both north and south. The trail passes through an open flat before disappearing left into the trees. Ignore a signed trail to the left, leading to the French Glacier, and instead follow the old logging road above Burstall Creek. This 3-kilometre stretch can be covered more quickly by riding a mountain bike on the slightly rough road to the braided stream crossing, beyond which cycling is prohibited. I remember being able to drive this road in the mid-1970s, scraping the oil-pan of my father's station wagon over protruding rocks.

Farther along the road, Burstall Lakes can be seen through the trees. Both these and Mud lakes attract people fishing for trout, though the best angling is earned by crossing Burstall Pass and descending to the Spray Valley.

At the end of the logging road, a rough trail leads down through trees to a broad dryas flats. The multi-braided stream channels here are created by glacial meltwaters that continuously deposit silts and gravels, around which the run-off must flow. Though some of the streams are crossed on boards, it's hard not to get your feet wet. The flats provide views to the south of these meltwaters' source, the magnificent Robertson Glacier, which rises in steps toward a col guarded by Mount Robertson on the left, and Mount Sir Douglas on the right. Watch for moose feeding in the willowy meadows between here and Burstall Lakes.

Across the flats, a trail climbs steeply through spruce forest above Burstall Creek, levelling out at the first stands of subalpine larch. Beyond is a long, open meadow filled in early summer with western anemone and yellow buttercups. The smooth limestone slabs that line the left side of the valley attract climbers wishing to practice their friction technique.

The small stream that flows down the middle of the valley is fed by a deep snow pack that lingers well into July. I once made the mistake of tackling this trip in mid-June and post-holed through knee-deep snow for a kilometre to the pass. As the trees are reached, the trail follows a depression along the left side of the valley and then swings right, rising over several limestone steps to reach Burstall Pass.

At the pass, one walks over deeply fissured rocks typical of karst landscapes. In some places, this grey "pavement" resembles the weathered bones of a large mammal. Near the west end of the pass is a large sinkhole, where the water has dissolved the limestone bedrock.

The views are splendid from this lofty pass, which straddles Kananaskis Country and Banff National Park. Looking back down the Burstall Valley, one can see beyond the dog-toothed Mount Birdwood on the left, all the way to the peaks of the Kananaskis Range. Far below to the west lie the bright blue waters of Leman Lake. It is a popular destination for backpackers, who continue over the pass, picking up a trail that descends steeply into the upper reaches of the Spray River valley.

The alpine terrain around Burstall Pass is a wonderful place to explore for several hours. While the adventurous can scramble up the ridge to the north, many hikers ramble through meadows in the opposite direction to South Burstall Pass, about 2 kilometres away. This lovely walk opens up views of the glaciated northern flank of Mount Sir Douglas (3406 metres), one of only two 11,000-foot peaks in Kananaskis Country.

SULPHUR SKYLINE

• **Rating:** Strenuous • **Distance:** 10 kilometres return • **Time:** 3–4 hours • **Elevation gain:** 700 metres (2300 feet) • **Topo Map:** 83 F/4 Miette • **Access:** From Highway 16, near the eastern gate of Jasper National Park, take the winding Miette Hot Springs Road 17 kilometres to its terminus in a large parking lot. The trailhead is just to the right of the hot springs entrance.

THE SULPHUR RIDGE is a no-nonsense hike that climbs relentlessly to a high, craggy ridge. The rewards are splendid views of a geologically ancient valley and, at the end of the day, a chance to soak sore muscles and sweaty backs in the hottest hot springs in the Canadian Rockies.

The first few hundred metres are paved, beyond which a wide gravel trail follows Sulphur Creek for nearly a kilometre. At an unmarked junction just beyond a drainage pipe, take the well-beaten track to the left as it rises through a forest of spruce and pine.

The trail levels out briefly at a low pass, where there is a signed junction. Straight ahead leads to Mystery Lake, but your route turns right and begins climbing in earnest up switchbacks. Pause to catch your breath at a clearing and look back down the Fiddle Valley at the Ashlar Ridge. This line of striking grey slabs, an attraction to skilled rock climbers, is composed of 530-million-year-old limestone.

The vegetation continues to thin as you climb, but the alpine terrain is by no means lifeless. In late summer, one can feed on succulent blueberries and listen for the rustling in the bushes of docile spruce grouse. You might also hear or see the tailless pika as it scampers through the rocks above.

Above tree line, the view extends southeast along the remote upper Fiddle Valley, its endless stack of ridges a wilderness explorer's delight. Once a level shoulder is reached, it's about ten more minutes of switchbacking to reach the summit. Then you're on top of the world with sweeping views north to the distant Moosehorn Valley.

If the skies are clear and the winds moderate, it's worth spending some time soaking in this marvellous view. The curious may also wish explore the lower ridge; if you do, be careful not to wander close to any drop-offs.

The return is a thigh-pounding descent down the switchbacks. Good hiking boots or shoes with plenty of traction are a definite asset in places where the pea gravel covers the trail like small ball bearings. When you're not watching your feet, enjoy the distant view across the Athabasca Valley.

Upon reaching the parking lot, one should definitely visit the hot and historic Miette Hot Springs. In 1919, striking coal miners built the original pool, which was expanded in 1937. Renovated in 1986, the facility has one hot pool (average temperature of fifty-four degrees Celsius) and one cooler pool, both with decks that allow views of the surrounding mountains. Thought by some early visitors to provide a cure for gunshot wounds, the hot mineral waters certainly offer a cure for sore hiking muscles.

ROWE LAKES

• **Rating:** Strenuous • **Distance:** 13 kilometres return • **Time:** 5–6 hours • **Elevation Gain:** 560 metres (1840 feet) • **Topo Map:** Waterton Lakes National Park • **Access:** From Waterton townsite, drive 10.7 kilometres up the Akamina Parkway to a roadside pullout and the Rowe Lakes trailhead.

OVERSHADOWED BY MORE famous destinations nearby, the Upper Rowe Lakes are, for my money, Waterton's jewel. The two alpine lakes are framed by a magnificent forest of larch that descends right to the water's edge. This is a wonderful outing in late September when the larch's soft green needles have turned to orange before falling to carpet the earth. The views are also splendid, particularly from a slabby perch

Overlooking Lower Rowe Lake and Rowe Creek Valley.

near the second lake that looks straight down on the lower lake far below.

As with many Waterton hikes, the trail commences on a moderate but steady grade and finishes with a steep trudge to a hanging valley. There are many diversions along the way, allowing for both shorter trips and additional exploration. While the lower lake contains some small brook trout, the fishing is not highly recommended.

Although the destination is the prime attraction, the Rowe Lakes trail is blessed with varied enchantments en route. It begins by briefly following lower Rowe Creek, which spills over a slick bed of red argillite, the colourful mudstone for which Waterton is famous. The trail then climbs higher and begins a long traverse left above the Rowe Creek valley. In quick succession, one walks across a flowered slope, a cool spruce and fir forest, and then an avalanche slope dense with vegetation such as cow parsnip and thimbleberry. Where the valley walls become steeply sided, notice how the low summits are covered in trees on the left and rocky on the right.

Beyond, the valley flattens out and Rowe Creek again becomes your close companion. It is a mesmerizing stream as it spins and foams around rocks draped in emerald mosses. On a hot day, enjoy this cool walk through forest, as much of the terrain above is fully exposed to the sun.

At 4 kilometres, a short trail branches left, crossing the creek to reach Lower Rowe Lake. Watch for hoary marmots sunning themselves on rocks just before the lake. The small lake is fronted by trees and shrubs and backed by steep cliffs, creating a sheltered spot that is perfect for lunch.

Until early summer, a waterfall plunges 150 metres down the cliff from a hanging valley above. Within an hour or two, you will be standing on the lip of that cliff. Rest assured, you don't have to scale the cliffs to reach it. Instead, you take a roundabout route, rejoining the main trail and following it for another kilometre to Rowe Meadow. This meadow is situated in a huge amphitheatre, the grassy slopes topped by high cliffs. It is a pleasant place to admire the many wild flowers—including Indian paintbrush, monkey flower, and bear grass—or to spend the night at the nearby campground.

Across a bridged tributary stream, a junction is reached. Take the left-hand trail, which climbs steeply up the side of the basin to reach Upper Rowe Lakes in 1.2 kilometres. Your pounding heart and aching calves will be forgotten as soon as the trail levels off and enters the first stand of tall larch.

The two lakes are just beyond, set in a magical forest of larch that makes this one of the most enchanting spots in the Rockies. The uppermost lake is guarded by cliffs, where bighorn sheep can frequently be seen. At the base of these sheltered cliffs, banks of snow linger well into July. The smaller, middle lake is a jewel ringed in larch and gnarled alpine fir. Follow the lake's small outlet stream along its slabby banks and tiptoe to the edge of a precipitous drop to the lower lake. The forested slopes of the Rowe Valley beyond have been carved by ancient glaciers into a classic U shape.

Return down into the amphitheatre to the junction. If time and energy permit, take the Tamarack Trail, which contours left around the basin, rising above tree line and finally climbing through red scree slopes to reach the saddle in Lineham Ridge.

This lofty, and often windblown, spot provides one of the most commanding views in Waterton. Across the valley, the three Rowe Lakes can be seen nestled in the forest below a long ridge. From here, the glacial action that carved the hanging valley containing the two upper lakes is clearly visible. Beyond the lakes, the views extend for kilometres across distant peaks. Directly below, to the north, are the three lovely Lineham Lakes, set in another hanging, glaciated basin. Don't get too close to the edge of this sheer drop.

Return to the main trail, descending the circuitous way you came up or taking a more direct line by running down scree and thrashing through scrub brush to the campground.

HEADWALL LAKES

• **Rating:** Strenuous • **Distance:** 15 kilometres return • **Time:** About 6 hours • **Elevation Gain:** 440 metres (1500 feet) • **Topo Map:** 82 J/14 Spray Lakes Reservoir • **Access:** From the Trans-Canada Highway, drive 50.5 kilometres south on Highway 40 to a junction. Turn right and drive 22.5 kilometres north on the Smith-Dorrien-Spray Trail to the Chester Lake parking lot. Alternatively, drive 45 kilometres south of Canmore on the Smith-Dorrien-Spray Trail. The trailhead is at the near, or south, end of the parking lot.

IF YOU WANT to pack a lot of variety into a summer's day and capture a feeling of remoteness, there's probably no better hike in Kananaskis Country than Headwall Lakes. Within a few kilometres, one passes through open hillsides, streamside forest, broad talus slopes, scrub brush, and larch forest. And the best is at the end—two small lakes hidden by "headwalls" of sloping grey rock.

The snows disappear earlier here, on the east side of the Spray Valley, than the nearby Burstall Pass, which lies along the Continental Divide. So this trip can be comfortably attempted by late June. The elevation gain is reasonably steady, with the biggest climb, up through scrub brush, occurring close to the lakes. The day can be shortened a bit by mountain biking on the lower approach trails, which double as ski trails in the winter.

The start is somewhat confusing, as the route follows a series of colour-coded trails that double as cross-country ski trails. Fortunately, there are route maps at each junction. Basically, over the first 5.2 kilometres, one follows this sequence: the blue trail for 1 kilometre, the blue-yellow for 0.9, the orange-yellow for 1.8, and the yellow for 1.5 to Headwall Creek.

From the parking lot, the trail parallels the Smith-Dorrien road before traversing right along the lower slopes of Mount Chester. As one rises on an old grassy logging road, views open up across the valley to Mount Burstall. The logging here that preceded the formation of Kananaskis Country in 1978 is evident in an old cutblock at the crest of a hill where wild flowers now bloom in early summer.

The trail descends to cross Headwall Creek and then follows the right side of the drainage through forest to an opening strewn with boulders. Take a break by hopping onto one of the large rocks and scanning the distant slopes for bighorn sheep or possibly mountain goats. Follow the creek across the boulder field and either contour right up scree slopes or scramble straight up through a ground-hugging clump of Engelmann spruce.

Just beyond, there's a lovely camping site framed by a tumbling stream and alpine larch. It's now only a short walk up delightfully smooth grey "pavement" (formally known as karst topography) to suddenly reach the first lake. The naked grey limestone that lies beneath your feet and angles up the adjacent slopes around this deep blue lake creates a surreal world perhaps unique in the Rockies.

Resist any temptation to turn around here and instead traverse around the lake's right shoreline, which often retains snow well into summer. Hike up a grassy headwall, bisected by the cascading Headwall Creek, to reach the second lake, situated in a cirque between Mount Chester and an unnamed ridge. I have seen a fly fisherman catching small cutthroat trout near the lake's inlet stream.

From here, there are views up the valley to the blocky summit of The Fortress, which overlooks the similarly named ski hill in the parallel Kananaskis Valley. Industrious hikers can explore for another kilometre or two up this alpine valley, past the source of Headwall Creek, to the base of The Fortress. Return the same way.

CARTHEW SUMMIT

• **Rating:** Strenuous • **Distance:** 16 kilometres return • **Time:** About 6 hours • **Elevation Gain:** 660 metres (2155 feet) • **Topo Map:** Waterton Lakes National Park • **Access:** From Waterton townsite, follow the Akamina Parkway for 16 kilometres to its terminus at Cameron Lake. The trailhead is reached by crossing Cameron Creek bridge to the left of the parking lot and small marina. • **Note:** Many hikers continue past Carthew Summit to Waterton townsite, which requires returning to Cameron Lake to pick up your vehicle or booking a morning mini-bus ride to the lake (contact Mountain Sunset Tours in the Tamarack Mall. Phone 859-2378).

THE TRIP TO Carthew Summit is a wonderfully diverse outing through dense forest, past lakes, and finally up to a high and brightly coloured ridge. From this lofty pass, one can gaze across the U.S. border to the glaciated peaks and alpine lakes of Glacier National Park. On a calm, clear summer's day, it's a wonderful place to go for extended walks along ridges composed of finely ground red rock.

Be prepared for a considerable gain in elevation, particularly at the start of the trip. But, like nearly all the Waterton trails, the path to Carthew Summit is superbly constructed and designed to ease the steepest climbs by means of switchbacks. Carry sufficient water, since this is a dry hike above tree line. Also pack some warm and weatherproof clothing. Carthew Summit is subject to sudden weather changes and exposed to the strong winds that often whip through Waterton Lakes National Park.

The trail begins by briefly following the east shore of Cameron Lake. The lake is a favourite destination for boaters fishing for trout or scanning the avalanche slopes of Mount Custer, at the south end of the lake, for grazing grizzly bears. Soon, the trail turns left through a 300-year-old forest of spruce and fir and begins switchbacking up a steep eastern slope. Heavy precipitation, particularly snow, creates ideal conditions for the growth of bush that is particularly dense on avalanche slopes. Indeed, Waterton is one of the few places in Alberta's Rockies to support such lush vegetation.

Still, there are glimpses through the forest to Cameron Lake, which becomes ever smaller as the trail rises. The trailside is also worth watching, for the delicate queen's cup and, near trickling streams, the lovely red monkey's flower. Higher up on rockier soils, there are clumps of creeping beard's tongue.

Finally, the switchbacks end and the trail climbs out of the dense forest. As the trail levels out, notice the ancient water ripple marks left in the red rock along the path. This stretch contains an unusual mixture of grasses, shrubs, and widely spaced whitebark pines and larch. Not far beyond is Summit Lake, a small body of water that supports a diversity of

Carthew Lakes from Carthew Summit.

wild flowers along its marshy shores. The lake sits on a forested plateau overlooking the Boundary Creek Valley which, not surprisingly, runs along the U.S.-Canada border. The dominant peak across that southern border is the glaciated Mount Chapman, its meltwaters feeding a row of alpine lakes at its feet.

The trail climbs above Summit Lake, then traverses to the right high above the valley floor, the mountain view south improving with the gain in elevation. Along the way are scattered alpine larch trees and clearings swept by winter avalanches off Mount Carthew. In summer, scan these open slopes for the tall and tufted white bear grass. Waterton is Canada's only national park in which this flower is found. As the name suggests, bears eat its leaf bases in the spring.

Coincidentally, after once passing one of these bristly flowers, I looked high up on the open slope near Carthew Summit and spotted a grizzly mother and two cubs grazing. Though I was more than half a kilometre away, she soon lifted her head, sniffed the wind, and leisurely moved her cubs over the ridge.

The trail traverses across the lower part of this slope and then carves a switchbacking line up through the red scree. Small markers indicate the route to Carthew Summit, a ridge overlooking Carthew Lakes to the northeast. The superb views from the 2300-metre ridge are enhanced by hiking north to the lower summit of Mount Carthew. But perhaps the most fascinating feature is the barren slopes of red argillite and quartzite for which Waterton is famous.

From Carthew Summit, a trail leads down through the fine scree to the two Carthew lakes. Many hikers carry on, dropping steadily to Alderson Lake and then walking through dense forest along Carthew Creek to reach Waterton townsite, an additional distance of 12 kilometres from Carthew Summit. But on a clear day, it's worth spending a few hours just exploring these lofty red ridges and then returning the same way to Cameron Lake.

CRYPT LAKE

• **Rating:** Strenuous to Advanced • **Distance:** 17 kilometres return • **Time:** 6–7 hours • **Elevation Gain:** 670 metres (2200 feet) • **Topo Map:** Waterton Lakes National Park • **Access:** The Crypt Lake trailhead is best reached by booking a return boat ride, which runs throughout the summer between the Waterton townsite marina and the other side of Upper Waterton Lake. Phone 859-2362 for more information on bookings.

CRYPT LAKE MAY not quite live up to its billing by a national magazine as the best hike in Canada. But few mountain trips anywhere can match the splendour and diversity of this day trip. Consider this exciting sequence of delights: a boat ride, a steep climb past waterfalls, a tunnel crawl, and an exposed bit of hiking to an exquisite lake enclosed by mountain walls. One can even walk around the lake and stick a toe across the U.S. border, without having to go through customs.

Hikers should be prepared for a full day's outing that includes a strenuous ascent of nearly 700 metres to Crypt Lake. Because most travellers will have to catch a return boat

Author standing above Crypt Lake.

ride in the afternoon, they should keep an eye on the time and turn around if necessary. They should also be prepared for some mild exposure on the trail near the tunnel, though any concerns should be reduced by the protection afforded by a short section of cable hand railing. Although a bear encounter is unlikely, hikers should make lots of noise while rising through the forest and up the steep valley.

From the marina, the motorboat ride takes only a few minutes to cross Upper Waterton Lake, which at 150 metres is the deepest lake in the Canadian Rockies. This depth is apparent when one reaches the dock at Crypt Landing and watches the lake bottom disappear sharply from view a short distance from shore. The sandy beach is a lovely place for a quiet picnic, best saved for the afternoon when awaiting the return ride.

The trail rises via a series of switchbacks along a forested ridge thick with fir, spruce, pine, and underbrush. Not far from the trailhead, a steep side-trail loops past Hell Roaring Falls, a detour best left for the descent. Instead, stay on the main trail up the Hell Roaring Creek valley, stopping at a viewpoint overlooking Twin Falls.

Two kilometres farther, Burnt Rock Falls tumbles in two thin braids over a lip of reddish dolomitic limestone rock that gives the falls its name. From here, the trail switchbacks steeply up scree slopes beneath Vimy Ridge, the views of the valley steadily improving with the gain in elevation. As you traverse this parched slope, look ahead to the end of the valley, where Crypt Falls tumbles down a steep headwall and feeds into a small lake.

A campground in the trees is passed at 7.9 kilometres, beyond which the fun begins. A trail across a steep scree slope leads to a natural hole in the rock enlarged to permit passage. Climb up a small iron ladder to the lip of the hole, scrunch down and squirm your way through the 20-metre tunnel. Upon emerging from the tunnel, scramble up and around an exposed corner, grabbing, if necessary, a steel cable bolted to the wall.

Back on easier ground, one passes a lovely patch of pink heather before cresting a small, forested rise. Exposed rock here has been weathered to resemble bleached bones. A short trail to the right leads to a small opening, where the underground outlet from Crypt Lake emerges and gathers its strength for the long fall over the cliff.

Beyond the rise, it's only a few steps through a stand of alpine fir and pine to reach the blue-green waters of Crypt Lake. The lake is situated in a hanging basin enclosed on three sides by high mountain walls that harbour mountain goats. Faint trails lead around either side of the lake, the far end of which touches Montana's Glacier National Park. Fishermen can try their luck casting for large cutthroat trout, while flower watchers can search for the rare pygmy poppy. Energetic explorers can scramble up the lower slopes to the west to gain a bird's-eye view of the lake.

It's tempting to linger in this peaceful amphitheatre, but make sure you have at least three hours to retrace your steps and catch the boat back to Waterton townsite. If time permits, take the short detour that descends steeply through open forest to a spot overlooking Hell Roaring Gorge. Look closely while descending the main trail in its lower stretches and you can often see bear claw marks reaching high up some trees. That sight may be sufficient to re-energize tired legs over the final few kilometres to Crypt Landing.

CORY PASS LOOP

• **Rating:** Strenuous to Advanced • **Distance:** 13 kilometres • **Time:** 5–7 hours • **Elevation Gain:** 900 metres (2950 feet) • **Topo Map:** 82 O/4 Banff • **Access:** From the west Banff interchange, drive 5.6 kilometres west on the Trans-Canada Highway and turn right onto the Bow Valley Parkway (1A).

Mount Louis from Cory Pass.

After 0.5 kilometres, follow the Fireside picnic road, to the right, to a parking lot at its terminus. The trailhead is on the other side of a bridged creek.

THE CLIMB TO Cory Pass is perhaps the finest alpine hike in the Banff area. Much of the approach is above tree line, rising along a ridge and scree slope to a rocky col frequented by bighorn sheep. This windswept spot provides superb views of the vertical upthrust of Mount Louis and the distant Bow Valley. The descent through a steep valley and cool forest completes this diverse circuit, which takes ambitious hikers on a circumnavigation of Mount Edith.

Be prepared for a sustained and often steep ascent as the trail climbs 900 metres in less than 5 kilometres. You'll need good hiking shoes or boots for the steep and rocky descent down the far side of the pass. Start early if it promises to be a hot day and pack lots of water, since none is available en route until the forested home stretch.

From the creek crossing, the trail traverses through a forest of mature spruce that opens onto an unusual and beautiful grassy hillside shaded by well-spaced poplar trees. In the early morning, watch for browsing deer or meditating hikers.

At a nearby junction, one trail proceeds straight ahead to Edith Pass, which is the way you will return. Unfortunately, your ascent route is left and straight up a bare, south-facing slope that will soon leave you gasping. A grassy knoll offers a good place to catch your breath and admire the commanding view of the meandering Bow River and the marshy Vermilion Lakes near Banff.

A little higher, the trail enters some trees, providing shade but no relief from the unrelenting climb. Finally, the route levels off as it follows the ever narrowing south ridge of Mount Edith. This forested ridge is departed by scrambling down a short span of rock and then swinging left to traverse along the right side of a drainage. The trail now emerges onto an open slope below Edith's south face and rises gradually to the rocky Cory Pass. Incidentally, Mount Cory is the peak to the west of the pass and is better known for the hole in the wall high on its south flank.

These barren and often chilly environs are forgotten as soon as the pass is crested, revealing the awesome south face of Mount Louis. Despite its impenetrable appearance from all sides, Louis is a popular and not overly difficult rock climb by its normal route, pioneered in 1916 by the legendary guide, Conrad Kain. Louis is a classic dog-tooth peak, its sedimentary beds thrust up on edge and eroded to leave highly resistant spires of limestone.

From the pass, the route drops sharply down a scree slope on a mercifully good path through Gargoyle Valley, so named for the rock formations along its sides. This rocky landscape is barren, save for a few clumps of dwarf buttercups alongside the trail and a tiny green meadow below. The trail traverses high beneath the north side of Mount Edith and then swings right, around its east slopes.

If the trail peters out when you reach a patch of scrub brush, you've probably gone too low. Head straight up and look for a trail sign and a well-beaten path. The trail now enters a moss-carpeted forest, a cool contrast to the stark landscape above. It crosses several avalanche slopes, including one where trees have been snapped like matchsticks by the powerful force of a sliding snow mass. From these clearings, one can look up at the steep east faces of Edith and its three summits.

The route now descends into mature forest, where the soft, needle-strewn floor is a relief to the leg-pounding of an hour earlier. The previous whistling of wind is here replaced by birds chirping, trees creaking, and a tiny stream gurgling through spongy mosses. It's now gently downhill all the way through a long stretch of forest to rejoin the Cory Pass trail about 1 kilometre from the parking lot.

TYRWHITT LOOP

- **Rating:** Advanced • **Distance:** About 12 kilometres return
- **Time:** 6–8 hours • **Elevation Gain:** 900 metres (2950 feet)
- **Topo Maps:** 82 J/10 Mount Rae and 82 J/11 Kananaskis
Lakes • **Access:** Drive 68 kilometres south on Highway 40
from the Trans-Canada Highway to Highwood Pass and a
parking lot on the west side. The trailhead is behind the out-
house, heading north.

THE TYRWHITT LOOP is one of the great hikes in the Canadian Rockies. Actually, it's more exploring than hiking since
there's often little or no trail to follow. Instead, you can design
your own route through this alpine wonderland. For the
ambitious trekker, this trip has it all: a high alpine col, a peak
to scramble up, an airy arch to stand on, two magnificent
ridge walks, and an intimate valley brimming with wild
flowers. Above all, there's a tremendous feeling of remoteness only an hour or two from the car.

The outing begins at Highwood Pass, which at 2200 metres
greets visitors with alpine larch as they emerge from their
cars. From the parking lot, briefly follow a paved interpretive walk before angling left through a grassy draw to a large
rock at its end. A well-beaten trail goes left up through woods
and over a treed ridge, marking nearly the only forested section of the trip.

Emerging onto an avalanche slope, hikers can pause to
look north along Pocaterra Creek to the jagged Elpoca Mountain on the horizon. The trail continues over a rock slide,
then follows a lovely stream enhanced by the presence of
pink paintbrush and emerald larch. Just beyond a small
pond, hikers should turn left up a grassy slope, watching
for a faint trail and cairns that lead to a rocky basin. Pick
a line along its left side and aim for the obvious col, or notch,
at the head of the valley.

It's a steep climb to Grizzly Col that can be tackled by

heading straight up snow, if it's present, or by heading left to intercept a trail that traverses the scree slope. The rocky col is often wind blasted, but it's worth a minute's chill to look back to the narrow Little Highwood Pass and to gain an overview of the terrain ahead. The col is aptly named, as two of us once discovered when we looked ahead to see two young grizzlies grazing in the meadows below, inspiring us to beat a hasty retreat.

From the col, the options begin. The fit and confident can scramble up loose rock to the nearby summit of Mount Tyrwhitt in less than an hour. Along the way, there's a large arch perched on the ridge, which is best admired from below because of a sheer drop on its other side. The 2874-metre Tyrwhitt, named for a World War I British admiral, offers superb views of the Joffre and Royal Groups to the west and the Misty Range to the east.

Back at the col, hikers face the choice of descending down into a meadowy valley toward two tiny lakes or staying high to follow a broad ridge to the left. If you take the former route, you can either round the ridge at its forested end or take a short cut back up to the ridge and pick a steep grassy line down the other side. Either way, you end up in a secluded, narrow valley, which in early July is filled with pale paintbrush, yellow columbine, and shooting stars. Larch grow along the cascading creek, and it's so peaceful you may be tempted to forsake a civilized existence for this paradise.

But there are more highlights to come. After hiking steeply up the grassy and bushy slopes, the ridge bounding the other side of the valley is reached. This long, high walk offers more extensive views, particularly of the Misty Range peaks to the east. The ridge continues to the top of a small, unnamed peak, where you might want to soak in the views one last time before descending. The descent down the north ridge towards the parking lot is easier than it initially looks. There's a trail down through the rock and scree, below which is a shoulder populated by pink moss campion and other mosses.

As a final choice, one can follow the ridge as it angles left or take a more direct route down grassy slopes and through gaps in the trees to regain the trail to the left of the parking lot.

Flowers and stream below Molar meadows.

CHAPTER TWO

Backpacks

Introduction

*I*n recent years, there has been a trend toward shorter day-hikes in the mountains. Still, some of the wildest and most magnificent country in Alberta's Rockies lies beyond the reach of average day-hikers. In the space of two or more days, backpackers can fully experience the diversity of Alberta's mountain parks—high traverses, forest walks, alpine meadow scrambles, and river valley rambles.

Sure, a strong party travelling light can often cover as much distance in a long day as a backpacker will in two. I've even heard of people completing Jasper's famed Skyline Trail as a day-hike. But these forced marches allow little time to enjoy the surroundings.

The sheer weight of a backpack forces one to slow the pace, to stop more often, and to let the mountain environment seep under the skin. As any photographer can tell you, the best time to see the mountains is at dawn and at dusk, when the light is soft and the animals are out. Such experiences are generally available only to those who spend a night or more in the mountains.

The best thing about backpacking in Alberta is the solitude. On many longer and more remote trips, one might see no other parties for several days. Alberta's mountain parks are generally vast enough to accommodate these kinds of wilderness walks, which can extend to several weeks without crossing a road.

At the same time, there are many fine backpacks on excellent trails. Indeed, one can walk for days in many parts of Banff and Jasper national parks without leaving well-beaten trails.

In sum, the combination of diversity, space, solitude, and availability make the backpacks in Alberta's mountain parks some of the finest in the world. Don't just take my word for it. Some of the most avid backpackers in our Rockies are from Europe and the United States.

Ratings

Backpacking is by nature a strenuous activity, requiring participants to be fairly fit and able to carry loads upwards of fifteen kilograms for two or more days. The five backpacks described in this chapter all involve elevation gains of at least 600 metres. Each crosses at least one high pass; several involve long ridge walks.

Strenuous: A two-day trip of less than 40 kilometres, on good trails.

Strenuous to Advanced: A trip of several days, covering longer distances but on good trails.

Advanced: A trip of two or more days, with considerable elevation gain. Route finding may be required.

Camping Procedures and Etiquette

Back country campers in the national parks must obtain a free park use permit from park information centres and warden offices or from the Canadian Parks Service regional office in Calgary. Back country camp-sites can be reserved twenty-one days in advance. In Kananaskis Country, registration is voluntary, which means camp-sites fill up on a first-come, first-serve basis. See the **Useful Contact Numbers** in the **Important Information** section at the front of the book.

Camp only in designated areas. In parts of Kananaskis Country where there are no designated areas, choose sites well removed from trails, water, and fragile environments.

Burn fires only in fire pits or other designated sites. Use supplied firewood or deadfall only and make sure fires are out before you go to bed or leave an area. Note: A lightweight back country stove is much faster for cooking and uses less resources than a fire.

Put all food and other smelly items (such as toothpaste) inside of packs, heavy plastic bags, or sturdy containers and put them up bear poles, where provided. Otherwise, hang food high up in a tree well removed from your tent. When above tree line, hang food off a high rock or at least bury it well under rocks, though rodents are apt to get at it.

Where back country toilets are not available, choose a site well removed from water. As well, wash dishes away from streams and limit the use of even biodegradable soaps. Pack out all garbage.

Backpacking Check-list

(in addition to the gear listed in the introduction to Chapter 1—**Hikes**)

- Sturdy two- or three-season tent
- Sleeping bag—Down or synthetic fibre, rated to zero degrees Celsius or colder
- Sleeping mattress—Either a closed-cell foam pad or a lightweight inflatable, the latter doing a better job of smoothing out bumps.
- Ground sheet (optional)—Protects tent against dirt or water leakage
- Backpacking stove, stove repair kit, lighter or matches

(kept in waterproof container), and fuel (usually white gas)

- One or two cooking pots
- Utensils—Cup, plate or bowl, knife, spoon or fork
- 15-metre length of rope—For putting food up a tree or bear pole; hanging clothes or sleeping bags to dry
- Flashlight or, better, a hands-free headlamp
- Gloves, toque, down or synthetic vest, thin long underwear—Mountain nights can be nippy

FISH LAKES

• Rating: Strenuous **• Distance:** 30 kilometres return **• Time:** 2 days **• Elevation Gain:** 755 metres (2475 feet) **• Topo Map:** 82 N/9 Hector Lake **• Access:** From the Trans-Canada Highway interchange just west of Lake Louise townsite, drive 24 kilometres north on the Icefields Parkway to the Mosquito Creek Hostel and campground. Park on the left in the roadside lot beside the hostel entrance, just before the bridge. To reach the trail, cross the highway and walk north over the bridge. A kiosk containing a map of the area is at the trailhead.

THE ROUTE OVER North Molar Pass to Fish Lakes is one of the finest and most diverse backpacks in Banff National Park. In the space of a few hours, one passes clear running streams, crosses a high and rocky pass, walks through an enclosed amphitheatre, and stands high above Upper Fish Lake and the remote Pipestone Valley beyond. Yet even all this splendour is overshadowed by a vast and magnificent alpine meadow ablaze with wild flowers.

Save this outing until late July or August, when the lingering snows have disappeared from these high meadows and the flowers are at their peak. The trip can be completed as a long day-hike but is best done at a more leisurely pace.

One can easily spend several days exploring the Pipestone Valley beyond Fish Lakes. The elevation gain is considerable but nicely spread out, with only one moderately steep climb, the final ascent to North Molar Pass.

From the road, the trail climbs through subalpine forest to reach a wooded bench that follows Mosquito Creek upstream. Despite the roots across the path, the walking is easy. Within a couple of kilometres, the trail drops into the drainage alongside the creek, necessitating some boulder hopping and crossing of tiny tributary streams. In winter, I have seen moose, up to their hips in snow, browsing on willow branches in this boggy valley.

Farther along, some moss-covered boulders are passed. Where these boulders have developed cracks, spruce trees have found a home for their roots, demonstrating the tenacity of life in a mountain environment. A forested campground, at 6 kilometres, is set amongst a lovely collection of such boulders.

The trail crosses the creek to the right and climbs an often muddy trail through thinning trees to reach a narrow meadow. Bisected by a tiny stream and filled with delicate wild flowers, this alpine gem is but an appetizer for what lies ahead. Ignore a trail leading right to Molar Pass and instead proceed straight for North Molar Pass.

Suddenly, as the trail levels out, the valley opens onto a rolling alpine meadow ringed by ridges of orange rubbly rock. By late July, the meadows, which extend for several kilometres toward both passes, are thick with purple fleabane, pink and yellow paintbrush, and various other species of wild flowers.

These lofty meadows are also fragile, so try to stick to the main trail. Unfortunately, heavy horse traffic, aided by hikers, has resulted in a series of parallel paths through the muddier portions of the meadows. In many such cases, the original trail becomes deeply rutted, often forming a channel for run-off waters. Horses and hikers naturally avoid these muddy ruts by creating a second trail and, eventually, a third and fourth. At such elevations, it can take years for the alpine soils and vegetation to recover.

In the midst of this basin sits Mosquito Lake, a shallow body of water supporting a patch of spongy green turf near its inlet stream. If you lose the trail here, go left around the north side of the lake, where the trail again becomes distinct as it rises toward the head of the valley. The last kilometre is a steeper climb through rock rubble and scree to North Molar Pass.

At 2590 metres, the pass is one of the highest on an established trail in Banff National Park. Not surprisingly, a bank of snow often lingers here throughout the summer. This rocky col provides excellent views west to Dolomite Peak and ahead down a narrow valley enclosed by rock walls. If it's early in the day and your legs are still fresh, you can drop your pack and scramble up through scree to a ridge overlooking the Pipestone Valley.

From the pass, the trail drops steeply, bypassing a rock slide fringed with yellowy green mosses. The lush meadow here is hummocky but perhaps even more striking than its predecessor given its contrast with the nearby rock walls. Unfortunately, the trail again becomes a boggy mess in spots as it descends to cross, on a good bridge, a cascading stream.

Just beyond, Upper Fish Lake is glimpsed below. For a stellar view, traverse right of the main trail on a slope that overlooks the lake and the distant, glaciated Cataract Peak (3333 metres). From here, it's just a short descent to the lake and the forested campground, your overnight destination.

While I have seen people casting for cutthroat trout in the upper lake, Lower Fish Lake was, ironically, closed to angling at last notice. Still, it's well worth the 1-kilometre walk to the lower lake, which is backed by one of the most northerly stands of alpine larch in Canada.

Fish Lakes provide an ideal base camp for exploring the surrounding terrain. A short walk to the north leads to a small lake and, just beyond it, Moose Lake. This high, traversing route offers a short cut into the upper Pipestone Valley. The name apparently derives from the nearby rock from which Indians carved their pipes. Those on longer backpacks can cross Pipestone Pass, headed for either Devon Lakes or the upper Siffleur River. The route passes a protected zone for woodland caribou, which summer in the high meadows.

An alternative is to head south and then east to eventually reach Skoki Valley. Most backpackers will be content to explore the immediate vicinity of Fish Lakes and return the way they came.

MYSTIC PASS—MOUNT NORQUAY TO JOHNSTON CANYON

• **Rating:** Strenuous • **Distance:** 37 kilometres • **Time:** 2 days • **Elevation Gain:** 580 metres (1900 feet) • **Topo Maps:** 82 O/4 Banff and 82 O/5 Castle Mountain • **Access:** From the

Hikers diving into frigid waters of the Ink Pots above Johnston Canyon.

Mount Norquay-Banff town turn-off on the Trans-Canada Highway, drive 5.6 kilometres up switchbacks to Mount Norquay ski hill, watching for grazing bighorn sheep and enjoying the lofty view of Banff along the way. Park across the road from the major ski hill parking lot and walk to that lot's far end to reach the trailhead, just beyond the ski chalet. Leave a second vehicle, or a bicycle if you're extremely energetic, at the Johnston Canyon parking lot, 18 kilometres up the nearby 1A Highway.

THE MYSTIC PASS loop offers an excellent tour of the toothy peaks of the Sawback Range and a backpack of sharp contrasts. The route begins and ends at two of the most heavily visited areas in the Banff town vicinity, Mount Norquay ski hill and Johnston Canyon. But in between are hours of rambling through remote and rugged country. The trip is also neatly divided into two parts: investment and reward. A long, level walk through forest the first day is followed the second by a dazzling succession of alpine lake, rocky pass, avalanche slopes, an enchanting valley, and finally a deep and narrow canyon.

While the trip can be tackled from either end, there's considerably less elevation to gain by starting from Mount Norquay. The trail begins gently enough on a dirt road that crosses beneath several ski runs, including the North American, one of the steepest plunges on the continent. Within a kilometre, the Mystic Pass trail heads left up into forest and traverses the lower slopes of Mount Norquay before descending an avalanche slope to cross Forty Mile Creek.

The ensuing walk west along the creek provides views of the impressive faces of, from left to right, Edith, Louis, and Fifi. These peaks are excellent examples of dog-tooth mountains, thrust up vertically millions of years ago, their steep limestone cliffs highly resistant to erosion but very attractive to rock climbers. The other major attraction of this stretch through forest is Forty Mile Creek, which flows enticingly between banks overhung by spruce.

As the trail follows the creek north for a long stretch, one has ample time to ponder the use of horses in the back country. In wet weather, the hoof-beaten track becomes a mucky porridge of boot-sucking holes intersected by tree roots. The trail, though, is fairly level as it passes through mature forest, which occasionally gives way to avalanche slopes and views of the valley.

At the 16-kilometre junction, take the trail to the left, which crosses Forty Mile Creek and swings behind a warden's cabin. The path is much better as it rises through forest to reach a clearing, exposing the Vermilion and Sawback ranges that frame the Forty Mile valley, now left behind. Not much farther, the trail crosses a small creek to reach at nearly 19 kilometres a well-placed campground, equipped with small picnic tables and bear-proof food caches.

The next morning it's just a short detour off the main trail to reach Mystic Lake, situated at the bottom of a large rock amphitheatre dotted with alpine larch. Back on the main trail, the only steady climb of the trip begins, a 300-metre-plus rise towards Mystic Pass. The appearance of larch signals an opening up of the valley and the beginning of the nearly 2-kilometre walk through the lovely alpine meadows of Mystic Pass. A cairn marking the height of the pass is a good place to stop and admire the rugged scenery and the folded limestone of the flanking Front Range peaks.

All too soon, the alpine meadows are left behind as the trail descends steadily past avalanche slopes, over streams, and across a boulder field. The last descent is through an open pine forest to a bridged crossing of a subsidiary of Johnston Creek. Within a kilometre, Johnston Creek itself is reached. Turn left.

You're homeward-bound now. After a little more than a kilometre through the woods, the valley opens to reveal the best views yet of the jagged peaks that give the Sawback Range its name. These mountains are composed of Devonian and Mississippian rocks, laid down horizontally beneath an ancient sea bed and then thrust up onto their edge some 70 million years ago. Subsequent erosion has created their sawtooth shape. Mount Ishbel, to the east, is one of the most striking sawtooth peaks in the Canadian Rockies.

Just ahead are the blue-green Inkpots, seven tiny ponds fed by springs that maintain the water's temperature at one degree Celsius throughout the year. A friend once dove into these frigid waters and shot out almost as quickly as he entered.

From the Inkpots, there's a final steady climb on weary legs to a forested high point. Unfortunately, all that elevation and more is lost as the trail switchbacks down above Johnston Creek. At a major junction, take the left-hand trail that leads to Johnston Canyon which, despite the hordes it attracts, is still one of the magical places in the Rockies.

This narrow gorge has been carved through the limestone bedrock over the past 8000 years. Near the top of the canyon are a 30-metre waterfall and a travertine drape, its brilliant yellow surface a combination of limestone deposits and twenty-five species of algae. In this vertical world is found one of only two nesting sites in Alberta of black swifts, which arrive from the tropics in mid-June. The descending catwalk has been bolted onto the overhanging limestone walls, leaving pedestrians suspended in places over the roaring stream.

The remaining few hundred metres of paved trail leads gently down to the Johnston Canyon parking lot and a cluster of tourist facilities.

BRAZEAU LOOP

- **Rating:** Strenuous to Advanced • **Distance:** 80 kilometres
- **Time:** 4–6 days • **Elevation Gain:** 640 metres (2100 feet)
- **Topo Maps:** 83 C/3 Columbia Icefield, 83 C/6 Sunwapta Peak, and 83 C/7 Job Creek • **Access:** The Nigel Pass trail-

Streamside flowers near Jonas Pass.

head is just off the Icefields Parkway, 8.5 kilometres south of the Jasper-Banff boundary or 3 kilometres north of the North Saskatchewan River bridge at the "Big Bend" in the road. The trail begins just beyond a locked gate.

THIS LONG CIRCUIT is one of the most complete and satisfying backpacks in the Canadian Rockies. It's a chance to spend up to a week exploring the remote country of southern Jasper National Park. Much of the trip is above tree line, including a long walk through a brilliantly flowered meadow and a climb to a barren ridge that is the summer home of the seldom-seen mountain caribou. Along the way, the route also passes a large lake and follows the Brazeau River along its broad valley.

Despite its length, this is one of the more popular backpacks in the Canadian Rockies. At campgrounds, one is apt to meet an international gathering of backpackers, particularly Germans and Americans. But the evening conviviality is often replaced by long hours of walking in solitude through this vast landscape.

The distance covered in this trip is eased by the good trails throughout. There are also lots of campgrounds, allowing parties to break the trip into a number of sections. If anything, this is civilized wilderness travel. As well, the elevation gains are well spaced by long stretches of relatively flat walking. While the trip can be completed in four fairly long days by fit backpackers, an extra day or two slows the pace and provides more time for exploring.

The first 7 kilometres of the trip, to Nigel Pass, fall within the northern reaches of Banff National Park. Unlike most alpine treks, this one starts by descending. The trail drops into the Nigel Creek drainage, crosses a bridge, and follows the valley up through avalanche slopes. There are good views along the way of Mount Athabasca to the west.

One soon reaches Camp Parker, a site long used by native hunters and by pioneering mountaineers. Many of the carvings on the tall spruce and fir trees have been left by more recent visitors. Look for a careful carving in the shape of a whiskey bottle. Beyond the camp, the valley narrows as it climbs north through heavier forest. A short walk left of the trail leads down to Nigel Creek as it cascades over its rocky bed.

The valley soon opens up onto meadows that rise gradually through stunted trees to the wide and naked Nigel Pass, which marks the entry into Jasper National Park. The orange chunks of rock here are of dolomite, while the distant slopes, streaked in orange and green, are made of Gog quartzite, the hardest rock found in the Canadian Rockies. To the right of the pass, the trail drops to cross, on boulders, the shallow south fork of the Brazeau River. Explorers with sufficient time might choose to take a side trip up this enticing valley to Cataract Pass.

The terrain is no less compelling straight ahead as the trail swings left around a long scree shoulder to overlook the main Brazeau Valley to the north. The elevation gained over the past few hours is quickly lost as the trail descends across old rock slides into a wet meadow and a bridged crossing of the Brazeau River. There is a campground just beyond, where Boulder Creek enters the Brazeau, but it's worth walking about another hour through the woods to the Four Point Campground. At 15 kilometres from the trailhead, this marks a good place to spend the night.

Rise early as the second day is the longest, and most rewarding, of the trip. From here, one must walk some 19 kilometres, including a climb over Jonas Shoulder, to reach the next campground in the Poboktan Valley. Begin by looking for a junction, just beyond the Four Point Campground, near a warden's cabin overlooking the river valley. Take the trail that leads left up Four Point Creek to Jonas Pass. Note: The trip can also be done in the opposite, counter-clockwise, direction from this junction, following the Brazeau River to Brazeau Lake.

The route climbs steeply for 2 kilometres through a forest of Engelmann spruce and alpine fir, passing several side streams along the way. Soon enough the angle eases and the forest is left behind for nearly the rest of the day. Ahead lies one of the longest and most magnificent alpine valleys in the Canadian Rockies. The walking is easy as you rise gently alongside Four Point Creek through a lush meadow that in midsummer is thick with wild flowers. The valley is flanked on the left by glacier-clad peaks and on the right by scree slopes.

Jonas Pass is a watershed dividing Four Point Creek and Jonas Creek, the latter heading northwest to join the Sunwapta River near the Icefields Parkway. Backpackers follow this creek for nearly another 5 kilometres of marvellous alpine walking before angling right towards Jonas Shoulder. The route up to the shoulder provides superb views down the Jonas Valley and beyond to distant peaks.

The shoulder, while barren, is the summer home of woodland caribou, known informally at these heights as mountain caribou. In late spring, these magnificent antlered animals migrate to alpine valleys to bear their young in relative isolation from predators such as wolves. Caribou, listed as threatened in Alberta, can often be seen along and below the ridge, though observers should maintain a respectful distance.

At a height of 2470 metres, the crest of Jonas Shoulder offers extensive views over Poboktan Pass and the lower, forested Poboktan Valley. Poboktan is the Stoney Indian word for owl, several of which were seen in the lower forest by the mountaineering explorer, A.P. Coleman, when he ascended Poboktan Pass in 1892. The pass has from ancient times served as a route across the mountains of southern Jasper.

From Jonas Shoulder, descend steeply through scree slopes on a trail that through much of the summer retains a snow cover. The trail proceeds north through alpine meadows to reach a junction with the Poboktan Trail and a campground. On a five-day trip, this is a good place to stop for the night. The alternative is to make this a very long day and proceed east over Poboktan Pass and descend steadily through a narrow valley to a small campground alongside John-John Creek.

From this latter campground, the trail continues through forest to reach an old rock slide path that provides views over Brazeau Lake, one of the longest and most remote lakes in Jasper National Park. The trail crosses a bridge over the north fork of the Brazeau River at a campground just below the lake. It is but a short walk upstream to gaze along the lake's 5-kilometre length.

The trail, however, follows the lake's outlet stream east for a short distance to a junction with the main channel of the Brazeau River. Here, one turns right and begins the long walk south along the Brazeau Valley. The trail initially climbs over a forested ridge and then drops to cross onto the east side of the Brazeau River. Beyond, it alternates between patches of forest and open meadows. This walk along the Brazeau River is but a small segment of the South Boundary Trail, a 165-kilometre, two-week trek through the remote heart of Jasper National Park.

The best place to pitch one's last camp is the Wolverine South Campground, situated in trees beside the river. The final stretch along the river is a lovely walk through open meadows that provide a distant glimpse of Mount Athabasca, at the edge of the Columbia Icefield. From Wolverine South, it's a 7-kilometre walk to rejoin the approach trail at Four Point Campground, and then another 15 kilometres back over Nigel Pass to the trailhead.

SKYLINE TRAIL

• **Rating:** Advanced • **Distance:** 44 kilometres • **Time:** 3–5 days • **Elevation Gain:** 820 metres (2700 feet) • **Topo Maps:** 83 C/12 Athabasca Falls and 83 C/13 Medicine Lake. • **Note:** A small Skyline Trail topo map set, complete with route descriptions, can also be purchased at the Jasper Information Centre. • **Access:** Drive 5 kilometres east of Jasper townsite on Highway 16 and then take the Maligne Lake Road for 45 kilometres to its terminus at Maligne Lake. The trailhead is just past a picnic parking lot at the end of the road. Leave a pick-up vehicle at trail's end, a small parking lot 6 kilometres up the Maligne Lake Road near Maligne Canyon. Many backpackers with just one vehicle hitchhike from the trail's end up to the start of the trip at Maligne Lake.

JASPER'S SKYLINE TRAIL is justifiably the most famous backpack in the Canadian Rockies. For more than half its length, the route stays above tree line, offering continuous and varied views over the wild country between Maligne Lake and Maligne Canyon. The alpine highlight is a 5-kilometre walk along the rocky ridge of the Maligne Range. On a clear day, you can see all the way to the Columbia Icefield.

This is one trip worth saving for good weather. The ridges and alpine bowls are exposed to high winds and subject to whiteout conditions. In bad weather, the views are obscured, and it's easy to get lost. I once spent a day trudging through an August blizzard along the height of the route, unable to see more than 100 metres and colder than I've been on many February ski trips.

Obviously, at elevations reaching 2500 metres, the snow-free season is condensed into a couple of summer months. Given the international popularity of this trip (I once encountered more Germans than Canadians), one should consider registering in advance (phone the Jasper Information Centre at 852-6786).

The Skyline Trail climbs more than 800 metres through a variety of terrain. Still, there's no technical difficulties involved on a route that follows established trails throughout. Anyone attempting it, however, should be able to use a map and compass in case the weather gets bad.

There are six campgrounds along the way, allowing backpackers to design a trip suitable to their pace and interests. Fit walkers can cover the distance in two or three days, while others will choose to proceed more slowly and explore the many side attractions along the way.

The first few kilometres are deluxe walking through lodgepole pine forest on a wide trail that quickly passes two small lakes, Lorraine and Mona, both said to contain brook trout. At 5 kilometres, a campground at Evelyn Creek is reached. Beyond, the trail switchbacks steadily up through Engelmann spruce and then alpine fir to reach the Little Shovel Campground at 8 kilometres.

Here, where the forest opens to reveal the Bald Hills, begins a 27-kilometre stretch of unencumbered views. The trail traverses past islands of stunted subalpine fir and climbs through rolling meadows to Little Shovel Pass, the first of three alpine passes crossed during the trip. The views are especially impressive of the Queen Elizabeth Range peaks, flanking Maligne Lake to the southeast.

The route descends from the pass into a lovely subalpine basin called the Snowbowl. Shortly after crossing Jeffrey Creek, the trail passes at tree line the Snowbowl Campground, which at 12 kilometres offers many parties a good place to stop for the night. The next campground, Curator, is 8 kilometres farther.

Beyond Snowbowl Campground, the trail climbs gently through one of the most stunning alpine meadows in the Rockies. The Snowbowl here is a huge amphitheatre, ringed by ridges and low peaks, which feed numerous small streams running down the flowered slopes. This meadow is often boggy and vulnerable to erosion from excessive foot traffic.

The trail climbs steadily to reach Big Shovel Pass (2300 metres). The two Shovel passes are named for the wooden shovels fashioned from trees by a pair of early outfitters, forced to clear a trail through deep snow to haul gear to Maligne Lake. In contrast to the lush Snowbowl, the far side of the pass is a barren landscape of finely ground rock interrupted by occasional clusters of boulders. Watch and listen for whistling hoary marmots here.

Beyond the pass, most backpackers take a high traverse to the right through this fine scree. Just past a side-trail to Watchtower Basin, a junction provides access via a short but steeply descending trail to Curator Campground. The campground is nestled in trees just above a horse camp and is a good place to launch the next day's strenuous trip along the height of the Skyline.

The climb past Curator Lake is the steepest of the trip, rising several hundred metres through a narrow and rocky valley to the corniced Notch. At more than 2500 metres, this is the highest point on the trip and along the entire Great Divide Trail in Jasper National Park. I once followed a moose's tracks through snow all the way over the pass, giving lie to the impression that these are only lowland swamp creatures.

Here, the true skyline begins. For the next 5 kilometres,

one walks on top of a high ridge, while gazing off at land-mark peaks such as Edith Cavell and Mount Robson and peering down into alpine valleys. These lofty bowls, usually headed by a small alpine lake, sometimes contain the big-footed mountain caribou. If you're lucky enough to spot (probably through binoculars) these shy animals, look for any that might be wearing bright radio collars, the legacy of a caribou study in the greater Jasper area.

Pay careful attention to your map here, particularly if snow obliterates the trail. All too soon, the ridge walk ends as the trail begins steadily descending from Amber Mountain to the Tekarra Valley just below Centre Lakes. Just beyond, Tekarra Lake is situated beneath the impressive northwest face of Mount Tekarra. A campground at tree line provides a good last spot at which to savour the alpine terrain above. The trail crosses an outlet creek below the lake and ascends through open stands of subalpine trees and then traverses around the shoulder of Signal Mountain.

Once, along this stretch, I saw a golden eagle attacking a marmot. Just beyond, in the middle of the trail, I discov-ered fresh piles of bear droppings and my singing voice (maybe this is where the term scat originated). A driving snowstorm had reduced visibility to almost zero, so I moved quickly along, hoping not to confront a humped shadow rising out of the gloom. The next day, back in the comfort of Jasper, I encountered two backpackers, who had left Tekarra Campground fifteen minutes behind me and had seen a large grizzly bear crossing the trail.

For most backpackers, this is a pleasant and uneventful walk with fine views of Pyramid Mountain and the jagged Colin Range near Jasper. Alas, the alpine odyssey soon ends as the trail drops to the forested Signal Mountain Fire Road. Shift your weary legs into automatic pilot for the final 8.5-kilometre trudge down to the trail's end at the Maligne Lake Road.

ASTER LAKE-THREE ISLE LAKE

• **Rating:** Advanced • **Distance:** 41 kilometres • **Time:** 2–3 days • **Elevation Gain:** 1200 metres (3940 feet) • **Topo Map:** 82 J/11 Kananaskis Lakes • **Access:** From the Trans-Canada Highway, drive 50.5 kilometres south on Highway 40, turn right and follow the Kananaskis Trail for another 13.6 kilometres to the Upper Lake day-use area. The trailhead is at the far end of the parking lot. • **Note:** You may wish to carry an ice axe and crampons for travelling along the edge of Northover Glacier, which can become icy as summer progresses.

THE ROUTE BETWEEN Aster Lake and Three Isle Lake is one of the wildest and most spectacular walks in the Canadian Rockies. It climbs past waterfalls, alpine lakes, and meadows and rises into the rocky heights where few creatures dwell. The highlight, if you dare, is a narrow ridge walk along the Continental Divide, looking down over a thousand metres into British Columbia.

Backpacker at Aster Lake.

While there is a visible trail for most of the route between the two lakes, the route is unsigned. It is easy to get off-route, even more so when snow covers the higher ground. Therefore, this is a trip for people able to handle a topo map and compass, especially if the weather socks in. It is also a trip for the fit and hardy. The trail rises some 1200 metres, easily making it the steepest climb of all the trips described in this book. On the rocky ridge between the two lakes, the winds can sometimes be fierce.

The trip begins gently enough by following the trail along the south side of Upper Kananaskis Lake for 5 kilometres. I once followed a young moose all the way along this rolling path. En route, a couple of bridged streams are crossed, including one that cascades down in a small waterfall, its whiteness accentuated by the surrounding mosses and forest. There are occasional views through the trees and across the lake to Mount Indefatigable.

Shortly after the trail turns north at the end of the lake, keep your eyes peeled for a tributary path that heads left through heavy forest. This trail leads in less than 1 kilometre to Hidden Lake, which begins to drain as the summer progresses. If you're in luck, the water levels will be sufficiently low to enable walking along the left-hand shoreline. The alternative is a miserable bushwhack higher up.

Beyond the end of the lake, a trail climbs steeply through thick forest to reach an open basin at tree line. Angle left up through scree slopes below Mount Sarrail to reach a thin trail traversing to the right below cliffs. This stretch is somewhat exposed, although the footing is good. Across the way, Fossil Falls tumbles down a rock face at the head of the valley. As the name suggests, there are many fine examples of horn corals and other fossilized remains in this area. Remember they are protected within Peter Lougheed Provincial Park and must not be disturbed.

The trail eventually traverses right, up through easy ledges to leveller ground above the falls. From this rocky spot, it continues through forest to reach a small and lovely pond, which by midsummer has often dried up. It is easy to get lost here, as the trail disappears, often luring backpackers to continue walking south along a tributary of Aster Creek. Instead, make your way across the rolling country to the right, using Aster Creek as a right-hand railing guiding you to Aster Lake.

Most parties choose either to camp near the stream or to push slightly farther to Aster Lake. Because the lake lies at the edge of tree line, it is often difficult to safely secure food. In any event, be sure to keep food well removed from your tent as this is bear habitat.

Aster Lake is a murky grey and the alpine terrain exposed to stiff winds, but the setting is rugged and superb. To the south, beyond the jumbled moraines lies the Mangin Glacier and at its head the snowy cap of Mount Joffre, at 3449 metres (11,315 feet) the highest peak in the Rockies between the U.S. border and Mount Assiniboine.

To reach the north side of the lake and regain the trail, Aster Creek must be forded, a chilly and sometimes deep crossing in early summer. Carry on around the west side of the lake, angling up and right to round the south ridge of Mount Northover. Follow a trail north through scree up a narrow valley to reach a col (grid reference 252041). Beyond, the route briefly enters into British Columbia as it traverses across a spectacular hanging valley that contains two tiny lakes, perched high above Joffre Creek.

Aim for the col just west of Mount Northover. You are now standing on the Continental Divide, at a lofty height of more than 2800 metres. Higher yet, to the south, lies Mount Joffre, named after Joseph Jacques Joffre, the commander-in-chief of the French army at the outset of World War I. The surrounding peaks—Lyautey to the northeast and Defender and Onslow to the west—also commemorate figures from the Great War.

From the col, backpackers face a decision. If the winds

are moderate and your nerves steady, you can walk the magnificent but increasingly narrow ridge to your left for about 3 kilometres along the Continental Divide. Be forewarned that the slopes on the left plunge more than 1200 metres to Joffre Creek, the equivalent of the elevation gained over the past day and a half. The ridge is departed at a col (221065) down scree slopes that lead north into a drainage leading to Three Isle Lake.

The other option is to proceed along the left arm of Northover Glacier, which can become icier as summer progresses. A small pass is crossed (238061) and the glacier descended northwest to reach a drainage, which is followed through a narrow valley and then braided stream flats to Three Isle Lake, where there is a back country campground.

The lake is named for the small treed islands in its midst. It is a popular destination for backpackers and fishermen, most of whom take the more direct route from Upper Kananaskis Lake. If time and energy permit after your long day, it's worth the 2-kilometre hike to reach South Kananaskis Pass and its views over the lake.

From Three Isle Lake, the route home heads east along the trail and soon descends steeply on switchbacks down a treeless headwall. Continue on through forest along Three Isle Creek past a fork (the trail north leads to Turbine Canyon, a worthy destination for another day).

Less than 2 kilometres beyond the forks, the Lyautey Trail branches right and leads to the approach trail around the south side of Upper Kananaskis Lake. For a different finish, stay on the north side of the lake, crossing a mammoth rock slide below Mount Indefatigable. From the Interlakes parking lot, follow the east shore trail back to the Upper Lake parking lot.

Canoeing down Bow River with Castle Mountain in the background.

CHAPTER THREE

Canoe Trips

Introduction

*T*he early explorers had it right. Canoeing is a great way to travel. Two hundred years ago, it was also one of the only ways to travel, as well as the easiest way to move furs and other trade goods.

Today, the canoe is slid into rivers almost exclusively as a form of recreation. Still, it's one of the best ways to travel and see the countryside. There's a unique perspective gained from the river, whether one is speeding through the mountains or floating in the midst of the city.

This is particularly true in the desertlike environment of southern Alberta. Where motorists see only bald prairie as they speed through, the canoeist down in the river valley is exposed to a rich and diverse ecosystem.

Paddlers also travel at a pace that allows them to see what those with a self-imposed deadline often miss. One of the great pleasures of canoeing is the ability to lift one's paddle, drift along, and observe nature. On a river, the pace is set by a current oblivious to human schedules.

In a similar fashion, the trips described in this chapter are largely dictated by the country they flow through. For that reason, there are no whitewater epics, where a premium is placed on highly developed skills. Instead, the emphasis is on the diversity of landscapes that Alberta's rivers flow through.

Perhaps the best geographical lesson one can take is to follow the course of one of Alberta's great rivers as it churns out of its glacial cradle, flows swiftly through mountains and foothills, and then lazily winds across flattening prairie. While no one trip described here encompasses all of these phases, collectively they embrace mountains, foothills, cities, and prairies.

Canoeing Ethics

The ethics of canoeing can largely be summed up as respecting the land and water you are travelling through. In other words, don't dump garbage into rivers or use them as convenient sewers, even if the waters you are floating on are polluted.

River access is fairly straightforward in most national and provincial parks and forest reserves. On the prairies and in the foothills, it can sometimes involve passing through private lands to reach the river, which is public property. In such cases, ask the landowner's permission to use private access roads and to perhaps leave a vehicle on private land. When using private roads, be sure to close all gates.

It is tempting to camp on any convenient gravel bar or other flat spot along the river. But remember that in national parks, only designated camp-sites may be used and a free overnight permit is required. Outside protected areas, pitching a tent on a lovely flood plain may indeed be trespassing on private land. If you're at all unsure, seek information or permission before you embark.

If you build a fire, do so in designated fire pits or, where possible, in established fire rings. Gravel flats well removed from vegetation and the river often provide a perfect spot to build a fire. Use only deadfall to feed your fire. A gas stove, while less romantic than a campfire, is a much more efficient means of boiling water and cooking food.

Ratings

This chapter assumes readers have some experience in river canoeing and have at least a rudimentary mastery of basic manoeuvring skills. If not, most canoeing clubs and many outdoor education programs offer courses in skills ranging from novice to advanced.

Having said that, most of the trips described here demand only novice-level skills. Even the two intermediate trips are not overly taxing and contain rapids that, for the most part, can be avoided by less-skilled paddlers.

This chapter follows the recognized international scale for rating rivers and classifying rapids. Thus the ratings for the sections described here are the same as those applied by the Alberta Canoe Association.

Paddler Skill

Novice Open Canadian—Paddlers can effectively use all the basic strokes from the bow and stern of an open Canadian canoe, can read water, and manoeuvre through Class I rapids.

Novice White Water—Canoeists are adept at all the basic strokes, can read water, and manoeuvre through Class II rapids.

Intermediate Open Canadian—Paddlers can also ferry, set and make eddy turns, line a canoe around rapids, assist overboard canoeists, and confidently negotiate Class II rapids.

Rapids

Class I - Easy—Waves are small and regular and easily navigated.

Class II - Medium—Waves are medium-sized and regular and passages are clear though they can be narrow. There may be occasional low ledges, sweepers, and log jams.

Class III - Difficult—Waves are high and irregular. Exposed rocks, eddies, and holes are present. Usually requires advance scouting.

Canoeing Check-list

- Canoe without a keel
- Life jackets, which today go by the term personal flotation devices
- One paddle per person plus one spare per boat
- Bailer
- Short rope attached to the bow and stern
- Canoe cover (optional) for white water
- Throw bag, containing floating rope, for rescues
- Knee pads—A cut up closed-cell foam pad works well
- Waterproof containers—Specialized bags, loosely knotted garbage bags inside a pack, or commercial-sized plastic olive drums (often available from specialty grocery stores and restaurants) with screw caps
- Large freezer bags or specialized chart covers for storing maps
- Packs—Waterproof or lined with a plastic bag, for storing gear. The straps allow them to be easily fastened to the canoe.
- One or two good lengths of rope for lashing down gear, lining canoes, and hanging up wet gear to dry
- Broad-brimmed hat, good sunglasses, and sun cream with minimum SPF rating of 15. Despite a cool breeze that often blows along river valleys, paddlers are exposed to the sun and reflected light off the water.
- Gloves (optional)
- Weatherproof clothing and an extra set of dry clothes and shoes—stored in a waterproof container. Remember to also keep your cameras stored in waterproof

containers, especially when launching into rapids or high waves.

- Old running shoes, sandals, or specialized aquatic footwear
- Pocket knife
- Adequate water and food
- Overnight Gear—The cargo space of a canoe allows overnight paddlers to carry coolers full of fresh foods and refreshments. For a detailed list of camping gear, see the backpacking check-list in Chapter 2.
  - Axe
  - Folding chairs (optional)

Canoeing Contacts

Alberta River Forecast Centre—Provides river flow rates on Alberta rivers from May through October. Phone 1-800-661-8917.

Stream Flow Fact Sheets—Shows average flow rates, including in a graph form, for various Alberta river stretches. Available from Alberta Environment, Water Resources Planning Division, 9th Floor, 9820-106 Street, Edmonton, Alberta T5K 2J6. Phone 427-8995.

HIGHWOOD RIVER—HIGH RIVER TO ALDERSYDE

• **Rating:** Novice Open Canadian • **Distance:** 23 kilometres • **Time:** 3.5–5 hours • **Topo Map:** 1:50,000 82 I/12 High River • **Access:** Drive 40 kilometres south of Calgary on Highway 2 to High River. Head west into town, turn right just before the railway tracks, and park on the far side of the bridge crossing the river. Leave a second vehicle, or bicycle, 22 kilometres north of High River on Highway 547 (just east of Highway 2) where a bridge crosses the Highwood River.

Paddling down the Highwood River.

THIS NEGLECTED STRETCH of the lower Highwood River makes for a fine outing in late May or June, when the water is high, the air redolent with wolf willow, and the river crowded with young families of geese and ducks. Indeed, this is a good trip for human families or novice canoeists content to lazily paddle down this gentle river while enjoying the rites of spring.

The Highwood, which begins life in the mountains of Kananaskis Country, is best known to canoeists for its challenging reaches of white water as it tumbles onto the plains. By the time it reaches High River, its fury is spent and it meanders as a small prairie river toward a merger with the Sheep River before emptying, not long after, into the Bow River southeast of Calgary. The section covered here is one of the few river stretches in southern Alberta to flow due north.

The canoe is plunged into the river in the midst of High River, the birthplace of Joe Clark and a historic centre of ranching and farming. In 1800, explorer David Thompson camped near here along the Highwood, which the Black-foot called Ispitsi for the tall trees that grew along its banks.

Soon, the town is left behind, civilization replaced along the banks by tall cottonwood trees that lend a sense of intimacy to this small river. Within a few kilometres, the vege-tation gives way to high dirt banks, which provide nesting sites for the hundreds of swallows that zigzag like bats above the water in search of insects.

The river, winding at first, takes more of a beeline as it heads north across the prairie. On many of these straight-aways there is little current evident, which can slow progress when battling a headwind. The good news is there's no danger to speak of, with the odd section of small waves and a few rocks to keep paddlers alert.

The best thing about this spring trip is the abundance of ducks and geese nesting along its narrow course. It's almost a surprise if you don't round a corner and scare up a cou-ple of mallards from the near bank. Unlike the webbed-foot creatures inhabiting the Bow River as it flows through Cal-gary, the waterfowl on the Highwood have maintained a semblance of wildness. The trick is trying to steer clear of the floating Canada geese, the parents trailed by a string of yellow fluff balls. Often mother and father goose will com-mence honking and flapping slowly downstream to lure canoeists well past their young.

While geese provide most of the entertainment, sharp-eyed paddlers might also spot soaring hawks, or elegant blue herons standing on their long legs in quiet backwaters. There are lots of places to pull over and watch the wildlife. You may also want to stretch your legs by walking above the river bank and gazing across the prairie farms to the distant mountains.

Despite the river's proximity to a major city and the busy Highway 2, there are few signs of humanity, including other canoeists, on this stretch of the Highwood. There is the odd irrigation pump and farmhouse along the way, but the only startling reminder of civilization is a massive meat-packing plant situated close to the river.

The Highwood eventually passes under a bridge on Highway 2, then continues over some slightly faster water for a few kilometres. Just past an impressive brick house, a high bridge comes into view and your nature tour is over. Beach your boat on the right-hand shore under the bridge.

RED DEER RIVER—DINOSAUR PROVINCIAL PARK

• **Rating:** Novice Open Canadian • **Distance:** 18 kilometres • **Time:** About 4 hours • **Topo Map:** 1:50,000 72 L/13 Wardlow • **Access:** Leave a second vehicle at Dinosaur Provincial Park, northeast of Brooks, and from the park entrance drive 34 kilometres on secondary Highway 876 North to the Steveville Bridge, which crosses the Red Deer River near the park's western boundary. Park in a picnic site northeast of the bridge and carry canoes through willows to the river's edge.

THE RED DEER RIVER is broad and slow as it winds through the spectacular badlands of Dinosaur Provincial Park in southeastern Alberta. The requisite canoeing skills are minimal, consisting mainly of steering a straight course and strong arming against occasionally gusty winds. This leaves plenty of time to study the dry prairie landscape and contemplate its interesting assortment of citizens—prairie rattlesnakes, toads, scorpions, black widow spiders, cottontail rabbits, cacti, and cottonwoods. Indeed, the slow pace of the river provides an excellent medium for imagining back millions of years to when dinosaurs ruled this once wet environment.

Many canoeists spend upwards of two days paddling sections of the river as it winds through the prairies from Red Deer to the Saskatchewan border. This short stretch through

Badlands in Dinosaur Provincial Park.

Dinosaur Provincial Park allows paddlers to sample some of the Red Deer River valley's finest badlands scenery in half a day. The rest of the day is well spent touring on foot the park's many delights.

This trip is best attempted in late spring or early summer, when river flows are at their highest, prickly pear and pincushion cactus are in bloom, and the heat is still bearable. Try to choose a day when the wind won't blow your boat upstream. Note: You must carry your own water as the river is unfit for drinking and the tributary streams are alkaline.

Canoeing down the Red Deer River through Dinosaur Provincial Park is straightforward. The current is moderate, bends in the river are sweeping, and obstacles are minimal. Just stick to the main current, following it gently from one side of the river to the other to maintain boat speed. As one drifts along, it's hard to believe this sluggish river bears the same ancestry as the Red Deer's upper reach, which delights white-water canoeists and rafters with its ledges, standing waves, and Class V rapids as it cascades out of the Rockies.

Some 14,000 years ago, meltwaters from the retreating glaciers of the Wisconsin ice age carved the broad Red Deer River valley here. Today's Red Deer is much smaller, its muddy waters carrying sands, silts, and clays washed into the river from the highly erodible landscape around you. As these sediments are deposited in slower waters, they form the islands, sand bars, and point bars that are common along the river.

Stop at one of these points, stretch your legs, and admire the giant plains cottonwood trees, one of the few forms of shade along the river. Dinosaur Provincial Park contains and protects one of the largest cottonwood river valley habitats in Alberta. Some of these gnarled trees are more than two hundred years old. But they may someday become dinosaurs themselves. The upstream Dickson Dam, built in the early 1980s, prevents the spring flooding needed to allow subsequent generations of cottonwoods to become established.

Cottonwoods aren't the only leafy survivors in this stark, desertlike environment where sagebrush and cactus flourish. The river bottom and tributary valleys support dogwood, willows, saskatoon bushes, and small birch trees. The river also attracts thirsty mule deer and airborne predators such as Ferruginous hawks, golden eagles, and prairie falcons. Venture out among the cacti and you might find a prairie rattlesnake curled under a rock or hidden in a thicket of brush.

The river valley is lined with hoodoos, which are sandstone columns carved by wind and rain into a fantastic variety of shapes. Hoodoos are a major component of the badlands, apparently a translation of a word used by early French traders to describe their feelings about the barren and intensely eroded landscape. This impressive badlands terrain, the largest such tract in Canada, is a major reason why Dinosaur Provincial Park was named a UNESCO World Heritage Site in 1979. From the entrance above the park, it looks like a miniature Grand Canyon.

Ironically this dry landscape was, 75 million years ago, at the edge of an inland sea where dinosaurs roamed in abundance. Their fossilized bones were preserved in the sedimentary deposits, which have since been carved into badlands. The rapid erosion of this landscape has helped palaeontologists uncover the remains of more than thirty-five species of dinosaurs, including hadrosaurs, centrosaurs, and Albertosaurus. Today, Dinosaur Provincial Park contains one of the richest dinosaur bone beds in the world, attracting visitors from around the world.

Because much of the park is closed to personal explorations, the best way to see its treasures is to take a tour or a self-guided interpretive walk near the visitor centre. That, incidentally, is the terminus of the canoe trip. Pull out at a small landing spot about 100 metres before the campground and haul your canoe up to a small building along a gravel road.

BOW RIVER—BEARSPAW DAM TO CALGARY ZOO

• **Rating:** Novice Open Canadian • **Distance:** 21 kilometres • **Time:** 4–5 hours • **Topo Map:** 1:50,000 82 O/1 Calgary • **Access:** Leave one vehicle or a bicycle in a parking lot west of the Calgary Zoo, near Memorial Drive east of Edmonton Trail. Drive the other just past Bowness Park on Bowness Road, turn left immediately north of the bridge and head west until the road is barricaded. From here, it's a short carry down to the river. • **Note:** Be sure to pull out before the weir, downstream of the zoo, which has claimed several lives despite all the warning signs. Life jackets are mandatory within the city.

WHY BOTHER TO lug a dusty canoe off the garage wall, shuffle cars, and then paddle through the heart of Calgary when you can cycle the same route in half the time? In a word, solitude.

Risk the river pathway on a weekend afternoon and you'll be constantly dodging strollers, cyclists, roller bladers, dogs, geese, and runaway infants. Plunge your craft into the Bow River instead and you can drift in peace with the current and wave like royalty to the miserable ants toiling on the asphalt.

They're a world away and so is the distant hum of traffic. Sure, you never quite escape the city, but what a different experience of that city. As it winds through Calgary, the Bow is flanked by parkland and poplars, the banks teeming with bird life and hopeful fishermen.

Best of all, surprisingly few boats ply this stretch of river that's an easy paddle for anyone who can manoeuvre a river canoe. The river from Bearspaw Dam to the Calgary Zoo is wide with broad turns and no rapids, sweepers, or big rocks to worry about. Still, in late spring and early summer, there's usually enough flow to keep you moving briskly along, with the occasional section of small waves thrown in for mild excitement.

Because of the numerous bridges, you can select your own entrance and exit points. For a pleasant half-day trip, start below the Bearspaw Dam. You'll soon be floating past Bowness Park, where for seventy years Calgary families have gone to skate on a man-made lagoon, enjoy amusement rides, and sit by the river. The park was donated to the city by a developer in exchange for a trolley line, which began carrying passengers to these outskirts in 1912.

A little farther downstream, Bowmont Park reaches from the north shore up high grassy slopes that in spring are covered in prairie flowers. The hillside is cut by several ravines, the largest of which contains several springs that spill down the slope. Just past a gravel crushing plant, the river takes a big bend to the right and passes under the double Shouldice Bridges before swinging left along Shouldice Park. The flat athletic fields found here were farmed in the early twentieth century by James Shouldice, who donated some of his lands to the city.

This first section of the trip is the furthest removed from traffic and the most densely populated with young families of geese, mallards, and mergansers. For this reason, you might choose to pull up early onto one of the many islands to walk around or munch on a picnic lunch.

Another potential stopover is Edworthy Park, where one can visit the old Edworthy house, look for traces of a long-gone brick plant, or enjoy a more formal picnic. A longer and steeper walk to the top of the escarpment leads past some of the most easterly stands of Douglas fir in Alberta. The observant might find traces of old Indian tipi rings on the plateau. Farther along the south shore is Lowery Gardens, an overgrown flood plain that in the late nineteenth century supported a market garden and farm.

As one nears the city centre, the strip of parkland on either side of the river gets narrower, with stands of trees shielding canoeists from the nearby traffic. Past the Crowchild Trail bridge, there's a fine view of the approaching downtown skyline.

The downtown core is glimpsed through the greenery of Prince's Island Park, which attracts thousands of Calgarians for musical and cultural festivals throughout the summer. The island's natural-looking east end—which harbours ducks, beavers, and the odd indigent—was ironically created when the park's lagoon was dug and the excavated material dumped here.

Before you know it, the Calgary Zoo is upon you and the watery trip through urban nature is over.

ATHABASCA RIVER—OLD FORT POINT TO HIGHWAY 16

- **Rating:** Novice Open Canadian • **Distance:** 20 kilometres
- **Time:** Allow 4 hours • **Topo Maps:** 1:50,000 83 D/16 Jasper and 83 E/1 Snaring River • **Access:** From just south of the

Rafters heading down Athabasca River near Jasper townsite.

railway station in Jasper townsite, cross the railway tracks and drive about 1 kilometre on Highway 93A. Turn left on Lac Beauvert Road and drive 0.8 kilometres to a bridge across the Athabasca River and the launch site at Old Fort Point. Leave a second vehicle, or a bicycle, where the Athabasca passes under Highway 16, about 20 kilometres north of Jasper.

THIS IS A wonderful, leisurely paddle through the broad Athabasca Valley, flanked on either side by the impressive mountains of the Front and Main ranges. The trip follows the route blazed by fur traders nearly two centuries ago as they crossed the Rockies.

The Athabasca is brisk moving and cold but contains no rapids on this short stretch north along Highway 16. Instead, the major challenge is choosing channels that contain the greatest flows. The river here is braided into a number of streams, which flow around bars and islands of gravel and silt deposited by the glacial meltwaters that feed the Athabasca. The fairly steady supply of these meltwaters ensures this section can be comfortably canoed in half a day throughout the summer.

The Athabasca River begins life near the Columbia Icefield and flows nearly the length of Jasper National Park before bending northeast and terminating its 1231-kilometre voyage in Lake Athabasca. One of its early tributaries, the Whirlpool River, descends from distant Athabasca Pass, which explorer David Thompson crossed through heavy snows in the winter of 1811 to find a route to the Pacific Ocean. For the next fifty years, fur traders continued to cross the Rockies here via the Athabasca Valley.

Indeed, canoes on this trip are launched at Old Fort Point, near where Henry House was built in 1811. It was the first such building erected in the Canadian Rockies and served as a stopover for passing North West Company fur brigades. The site is now a pleasant place to take a nature walk and a popular exit off the river for upstream rafting tours.

Once the canoe trip is under way, paddlers soon notice the growing breadth of the Athabasca Valley, which was brimming with ice during the last period of glaciation. Towards the end of that ice age, the valley was filled by a mammoth lake that deposited sediments, now evident as forested benches along the base of the valley's mountains. Today, the valley is one of the lowest in the Canadian Rockies and supports a dry montane forest that attracts deer and elk.

The river soon passes close to Lac Beauvert and Jasper Park Lodge, built by Canadian National Railway in the early 1920s and still one of the most fashionable resorts in the mountain parks. At one time, the Grand Trunk Pacific ran a competing line up the Athabasca Valley; its former right-of-way now underlies part of Highway 16 to the northeast.

A couple of kilometres farther, the Athabasca passes under a bridged road that leads to the much-photographed Maligne Lake. A short while later, the Maligne River enters the Athabasca after tumbling through its magnificent canyon. Here is a good example of a hanging valley, where retreating glaciers have left the Maligne Valley dangling high above its intersection with the Athabasca Valley.

As one paddles lazily along, there are lots of opportunities to admire the parade of passing mountains. Unlike the Jasper-Banff highway, this valley cuts across the end of the mountain ridges, revealing a different and varied geological perspective. To the right, the grey limestone of the Colin Range has been thrust up on its edge and eroded into the distinctive jagged pattern of sawtooth mountains. Across the valley to the left is a prominent Jasper landmark, the orange-brown quartz sandstones of Pyramid Mountain. To its immediate north rise the impressive limestone cliffs of the Palisade which, despite its proximity to Pyramid, is some 250 million years younger and part of the Front Ranges.

At 15 kilometres, you can beach your canoe, stretch your legs, and walk up the bank to an open field. Here are the old log cabins erected in 1898 by Ewan Moberly, who, along with his brother John, was one of the early settlers in the valley.

Back on the river, the swift Snaring River soon enters the Athabasca from the left. Ahead and to the right, Morro Peak marks the end of the Colin Range. On warm days, watch for climbers ascending routes on its west face.

The trip ends nearby where Highway 16 crosses the Athabasca. Not far along the highway, Cold Sulphur Spring emerges from the rock, carrying with it the pungent smell of hydrogen sulphide. Admire the fossils in the bedrock here but remember it's illegal to disturb or remove them.

Many paddlers carry on for about 5 more kilometres to Jasper Lake, but its numerous sandbars can force canoeists to drag their boats during low water. Over the years, blowing sands have formed dunes that have separated Jasper Lake from the smaller Talbot Lake. The highway follows the narrow course between the two lakes.

At the north end of Jasper Lake is a sign commemorating Jasper House, named after Jasper Hawes, the factor of this North West Company fur trade post. Jasper House was built along Brule Lake to the northeast in 1813 and moved to this site in 1829 after the North West Company was swallowed by the rival Hudson's Bay Company.

MILK RIVER

• **Rating:** Novice Open Canadian • **Distance:** 62 kilometres • **Time:** 2–3 days • **Topo Maps:** 1:50,000 82 H/1 Milk River and 72 E/4 Coutts • **Access:** Drive about 5 kilometres south of the town of Milk River on Highway 4, turn left onto a gravel road and drive down a hill to a municipal campground to gain access to the river. Leave a second vehicle in Writing-On-Stone Provincial Park campground, 42 kilometres east of Milk River on Highway 501.

THE MILK IS A magical river as it winds through a unique, desertlike landscape along Alberta's southern boundary. Here, as one paddles through narrow sandstone walls in the land of rattlesnakes and antelope, there is a sense of

Looking over Milk River to distant Sweetgrass Hills in Montana.

wilderness and intimacy experienced on few Alberta rivers. You might even feel a connection with the Indians who carved their stories in rock centuries ago.

This is a great weekend trip in June or early July, when the cacti are in bloom and the shallow river swells to cover most of the rocks. The canoeing is enjoyable yet sufficiently challenging for novices to test their skills on Class I rapids and the many swings in the river. But on the Milk, a canoe is primarily a vehicle for transporting visitors through a fascinating landscape largely invisible to the landlocked traveller.

The Milk is Alberta's only south-flowing river. It rises out of northern Montana and crosses into Alberta, hugging the U.S. border as it heads east through thinly populated prairie. The river then departs south, its murky waters eventually reaching the Gulf of Mexico via the Missouri and Mississippi rivers. Canoeists are advised to carry their own water.

Almost as soon as their boats dip into the water, canoeists become absorbed in the intimacy of this narrow valley. At first, they focus on the tortuous course of the river, which reveals new enchantments around every sharp corner. Then, as they get a feel for the channel, their senses open to the smells of sagebrush and the delicate hues of vetches. Not far downstream, hundreds of swallows emerge from crevices in the banks and swoop, like aspiring extras in a Hitchcock film, above ducking paddlers.

About 19 kilometres downstream, the banks of clay and gravel are replaced by walls of sandstone that shut the valley off from the irrigated farms and ranches above. In some places, the current has cut into the soft rock and canoeists must guard against being swept into a wall. But if inattention causes a boat to overturn or founder on a rock, it's usually easy wading in fairly warm waters to shore.

There are numerous places to pull over and camp, but be careful not to encroach on private property. Where possible, it's worth walking to hilltops above the valley, where one can gaze down on the curving river and, in the distance, see the Sweetgrass Hills rising from the Montana prairie. Look the other way across broad fields and you might spot browsing deer or antelope. We once saw a golden eagle learning to fly as it coasted down from the cliff toward the river and then lumbered on foot back to its launching pad. On any exploratory rambles, wear shoes or boots in case you step on a thorny cactus or, worse, a rattlesnake.

Such camp-sites along the river were also used for centuries by Indians. In places, vestiges of their hearths and tipi rings are still evident, as are the petroglyphs they inscribed on the soft sandstone walls.

At about 40 kilometres, the sandstone has been carved by the elements into hoodoos and tablerocks, the latter having a hard cap over an intricately eroded base. Too soon, the intimate sandstone cliffs are left behind, opening the valley to a more prairielike landscape frequented by cows. Immediately past the last cliffs, a broad valley called Verdigris Coulee extends back to the left. On the top of an isolated sandstone rock in the middle of this depression, we once saw a huge raptor's nest with half a dozen fluffy heads poking above the branches.

Upon entering the prairie, the river becomes straighter and slower, requiring some muscle if a headwind is encountered. The landscape here is dominated by cottonwood stands and grazing cattle. More than one hundred years ago, the cow's predecessor, the bison, roamed these grasslands. As evidence of that lost heritage, I once saw a young couple on an inner tube dragging a buffalo skull they had unearthed from a muddy bank.

Not far past a bridge, the river takes a couple of sluggish bends, passes a rodeo grounds, and then reaches its terminus at the Writing-On-Stone Provincial Park campground, an oasis of shady green in this arid landscape. Here, the Indians' mysterious rock art has been preserved in the form of petroglyphs—carvings etched into the rock—and pictographs—paintings made from a combination of red ochre, water, and animal grease. Writing-On-Stone contains hundreds of scenes depicting such things as stick figures, hunters on horses, and shield-bearing men. These ancient sites are protected and can only be toured in the company of an interpreter. After leaving the relative cool of the river, canoeists may find this desertlike tour intensely hot. Even the rattlesnakes have shed their skins.

Across the river, a North West Mounted Police outpost has been reconstructed. The original outpost was established a century ago to maintain law and order along the border and especially to discourage the passage of U.S. whisky traders.

As you drive up and out of the park, turn around for a last look at one of the finest views of hoodoo formations in southern Alberta.

BOW RIVER—LAKE LOUISE TO REDEARTH CREEK

• **Rating:** Intermediate Open Canadian (Novice Open Canadian if rapids portaged) • **Distance:** 40 kilometres • **Time:** About 5 hours • **Topo Maps:** 1:250,000 82 N Golden and 82 O Calgary; 1:50,000 82 N/8 Lake Louise, 82 O/5 Castle Mountain, and 82 O/4 Banff • **Access:** Park either at the bridge over the Bow River 3 kilometres south of the Lake Louise interchange or at a clearing along the river another kilometre south. Leave a second vehicle or bicycle at the Redearth Creek picnic area, 9.7 kilometres south of Castle Junction on the east side of the Trans-Canada Highway.

THE BOW RIVER below Lake Louise is a fast-moving, glacier-fed river that is a delight to paddle. Still wild and clean in its upper reaches, the milky Bow winds down a broad valley framed by a succession of peaks. Even the occasional encroachment of traffic along the Trans-Canada

Highway is but a reminder of how much nicer it is to be floating downstream than simmering behind a line of motorhomes. Other than two short sets of rapids, both avoidable, this stretch of river is relatively easy to paddle. Yet the constantly shifting channel and patches of small waves will keep paddlers on their toes throughout this short day-trip. You might try your luck at fishing.

From the outset, there's a choice to make. You can go for the excitement of Class II rapids (Class III at high water and IV at very low water) right beneath the bridge south of Lake Louise. Or you can drive another kilometre downstream and ease into a considerably gentler flow. The only other choices along the way are picking the right channels around the many islands. Wherever possible, stick to the main channel.

Beyond the Louise rapids, the only real danger is posed by occasional sweepers, which are trees or logs extending from the river's banks, waiting to snare unsuspecting canoeists. For the most part, the leaning spruce are high enough above the water to allow clear passage. But paddlers must remain vigilant. I almost got an unwanted hair cut after carelessly swinging too close to an inside corner.

Because the Bow is glacier fed, the river flow is usually sufficient throughout the summer to cover most rocks and keep canoes moving smartly. The glacial meltwater—carrying sands, silts, and gravels—accounts for the river's milky green colour, which becomes clearer in fall when the run-off subsides. For these reasons, fishing for trout or rocky mountain whitefish is at its best before or after run-off, when the water is clearest.

The early paddling takes canoeists past the impressive east ridge of Mount Temple, which at 3543 metres (11,624 feet) is the third highest peak in Banff National Park. Closer at hand, the Bow River flows through a montane forest of lodgepole pine, with spruce growing closer to the banks. As you paddle, watch for merganser ducks riding the current, kingfishers, and perhaps a bald eagle flying along the river. You might even spot a watering moose hip deep in placid backwaters.

About two hours downstream, a small island in the centre of the channel is reached. It's a good place to stretch your legs and have a bite to eat amongst the wild flowers.

Not far beyond this rest stop, the long and impressive flanks of Castle Mountain swing into view on the left. The steep limestone and dolomite buttresses that rise from half-way up the southwest face offer a popular challenge for rock climbers. See if you can spot the tiny alpinists' hut on a broad ledge halfway up the mountain. The low gap across the valley marks Vermilion Pass, up which Highway 93 winds en route to the Windermere Valley. The peak on its left is Storm Mountain, which stands some 400 metres higher than Castle.

At the end of the long Castle Mountain, canoeists can cut the trip short by pulling out at Castle Junction, where the river passes beneath a bridge crossing the 1A Highway. Those who carry on should take care not to get sidetracked on a long side channel to the left, instead steering for the main channel on the right that closely follows the Trans-Canada Highway. While the side channel is sufficiently deep to navigate, it is somewhat narrower, with some sweepers extending almost all the way across the water.

The stretch of river below Castle Junction provides superb views of the aptly named Sawback Range. The most impressive of these jagged peaks is nearby Mount Ishbel, its long, uneven ridge running above clusters of limestone teeth. The prominent peak on the other side of the valley is Pilot Mountain, which rises in steps to a narrow summit.

About 11 kilometres, or one hour of paddling, below Castle Junction, the end of the trip is reached at the Redearth Creek picnic site. Pull out on the right in a quiet pool of water just past a portage sign.

Intermediate paddlers who want to end the trip with a flourish, can run the Redearth Creek Rapids, which are Class II at high water and III at lower water. They should be scouted for difficulty and exposed rocks. These rapids can also be portaged on the right.

For a longer trip, carry on downstream, where the channel becomes slower, more braided, and more exposed to sweepers. Exit either at the double bridge over the Trans-Canada Highway before Banff or near the boat-house in Banff. On no account, should canoeists proceed farther as the plunge over the Class VI waters of Bow Falls, beneath the Banff Springs Hotel, is apt to be fatal.

NORTH SASKATCHEWAN RIVER—HORBURG TO BRIERLEY RAPIDS

• **Rating:** Intermediate Open Canadian or Novice White Water • **Distance:** 40 kilometres • **Time:** About 5 hours • **Topo Maps:** 1:250,000 83 B Rocky Mountain House; 1:50,000 83 B/6 Crimson Lake, and 83 B/7 Rocky Mountain House • **Access:** Drive about 25 kilometres west of Rocky Mountain House on Highway 11 and then take a gravel road 4 kilometres southwest to the former town of Horburg. Alter-

Brierley Rapids on the North Saskatchewan River.

natively, take the more scenic road along the river from Rocky Mountain House to Horburg. At Horburg, drive down a short road to the river. Leave a second vehicle in a parking lot beside Rocky Mountain House National Historic Site, reached by driving south on 11A and then east along the river.

THE NORTH SASKATCHEWAN River from Horburg to Brierley Rapids is justifiably one of central Alberta's favourite river runs. The river is clear, fast, and sufficiently varied to please a diversity of paddlers as it flows through foothills forest. Intermediate canoeists can plunge through several sets of Class II rapids, while the less-experienced can steer clear of these rough waters. In either case, there's plenty of time to enjoy floating down a river that was once a major transportation corridor for natives, explorers, and fur traders.

Ironically, the river's character, which makes it so enjoyable for the average canoeist, is very much shaped by the hand of man. Indeed, the explorers of two hundred years ago would scarcely recognize this stretch of river. The construction upstream of the Bighorn Dam has eliminated some powerful rapids and filtered out water-borne sediments, resulting in a clearer, tamer river. The river flows are consequently more consistent, allowing this run to be enjoyably canoed from late spring through the fall. It's an ideal trip on a warm day in mid-September, when the aspen leaves are brilliant yellow.

Although this trip can be comfortably completed in a short day, it lends itself nicely to an overnight outing. Canoeists can spend the night at a forest service campground near Horburg or at one of several gravelly camp-sites along the river, where there's generally lots of driftwood for camp-fires. Once off the water, they can spend some time touring Rocky Mountain House National Historic Site.

The North Saskatchewan is typical of central Alberta rivers as they move through the transition zone from foothills to parkland forest. Its valley is fairly shallow with occasional outcrops of shale and stratified mudstones along its banks. The river is characterized by numerous cutbanks, sweeping bends, rapids, and long straightaways lined with beaches. The North Saskatchewan is considerably gentler here than in the suicidal canyons near its Saskatchewan Glacier source in northern Banff National Park.

In spring and early summer, the river is alive with ducks and geese. With luck, you might spot a beaver emerging from its river lodge. The surrounding forest is home to moose, deer, and elk, best seen at dusk or dawn, when they come down to the river to drink. I've heard of one group of twilight paddlers who had to back paddle furiously to avoid hitting elk crossing the river.

Still, this is not a wilderness paddle. Acreages and some farms are visible along the way, and the river is paralleled by a derelict CNR rail line, which once served upstream coal mines near Nordegg. Coal mining in this foothills region has generally been replaced by the production of sour gas, which is cleaner burning but toxic in its natural state. The river itself is often busy with canoeists and with fishermen, who cast from shore for trout and rocky mountain whitefish.

The launch at Horburg is on a shallow, secondary channel. Unless you want to bump along the bottom, it's best to pull your boat upstream or downstream to reach the main channel. About 5 kilometres downriver, the Devil's Elbow rapids are reached on an inverted U-bend in the river. The once enormous standing waves have been replaced in the post-dam era with smaller rollers and waves that can still reach 2 metres at high water. By staying to the inside curve before the bend, less ambitious paddlers will encounter much smaller waves.

Below Devil's Elbow are several well-spaced rapids. The first is Old Stony (6.5 kilometres downstream), named for a large rock in mid-channel. Two kilometres past a pipeline right-of-way, canoeists encounter the two-part Fisher's

Rapids. The first part, a series of boulders, can be avoided on the right. The second part, around the next left-hand corner, is a set of standing waves extending diagonally across two-thirds of the river; these can be bypassed along the left bank. Five kilometres downstream are found the standing waves of Grier Rapids, which can be avoided on the left.

About 1.5 kilometres later, the Brierley Rapids, on the right channel around a gravel island, signal the end of the trip. There is a good pull-out on the left above the rapids. A series of ledges at Brierley create large standing waves, attracting advanced canoeists and kayakers, who often spend hours honing their skills in the white water. These rapids have been the site of many kayak slalom competitions.

Once on shore, it's a short walk on rubbery legs to Rocky Mountain House National Historic Site. It marks the site of the last Rocky Mountain House trading post, which closed in 1875. The original post was built slightly downstream in 1799 by the North West Company. The fort was closed three years later after the Norwesters, along with the rival Hudson's Bay Company, were unsuccessful in convincing the Kootenay Indians to cross the mountains and trade with them. Rocky Mountain House briefly served as the headquarters for David Thompson's forays across the mountains and it later launched York boats carrying trade goods on the North Saskatchewan to Lake Winnipeg.

Cyclist on Elbow Loop road with Mount Romulus in the back-ground.

CHAPTER FOUR

Mountain Bike Trips

Introduction

*I*n many respects, the mountain bike is a great invention. Principally, it allows outdoor enthusiasts to travel great distances in a short time. A bike is particularly valuable on long, flat fire roads that can be drudgery to walk. Theoretically, the speed of a mountain bike allows its users more time to enjoy the scenery.

Unfortunately, like many time-saving devices, a mountain bike can often just speed up expectations or encourage marathon trips. Thus, speed freaks arriving at an alpine lake before noon might be tempted to race back to civilization for a late afternoon cappuccino. Like telemark skiing or white water canoeing, mountain biking can also be exhilarating. But one hopes it never reaches the point where the thrill of the sport, with a mountain backdrop, overshadows the experience of the mountain environment.

The other conundrum of mountain biking is more philosophical. Much as a helicopter can put any mountain destination within a half-hour's reach, so too can a mountain bike turn wilderness access into a short day-trip. To a certain extent, this question has been answered, for now, by restricted use of mountain trails in the mountain national parks.

While Banff, Jasper, and Waterton national parks may boast more famous sights and hikes, Kananaskis Country has these old-timers licked when it comes to mountain biking trails. This provincial recreation area is perfectly suited to the sport, having many old logging and mining roads, long, low ridges and much fewer restrictions on the use of mountain bikes. As evidence, there are nearly one hundred recognized bike routes in Kananaskis Country, three times the combined number offered by Alberta's mountain national parks.

Theoretically, any trail that can be hiked can be mountain biked. But trails that climb steeply and steadily, follow excessively rootbound trails, or cross long stretches of boulder fields or scree slopes are generally unsuitable for mountain biking. Yet many times when, on foot, I think a trail is unridable, I see the tracks of an intrepid cyclist.

Riding Ethics

The mountain bicycle is the latest addition to the mix of mountain trail users. As the only mechanical device allowed on most trails, bikes, and their riders, must be governed by certain rules if their use is to become accepted on a long-term basis in the back country.

The first rule of mountain biking is to respect other trail users. People come to the mountains to escape the rush of civilization. The last thing they want is to be scared out of their wits by a kamikaze rider screeching around a corner or racing down a hill towards them. When riding a mountain bike, keep your speed in check, especially when rounding corners or cresting hills. Slow down when you see hikers and pull right over and dismount when passing horses, so as not to frighten them. If possible, stand on the downhill side of approaching horses. Announce your approach to all trail users well in advance by sounding your bike bell.

Horses aren't your biggest worry in the back country. Because of the speed and relative quiet of their travel, mountain bikers are more apt than hikers to startle bears, with unpredictable results. More than one cyclist has been mauled by a surprised mother grizzly or black bear. For that reason, bikers should sound their bells or, better yet, yell at frequent intervals, especially when coming around corners, topping hills, travelling in heavy forest, riding into a strong wind, or when following or nearing a noisy stream. Cyclists should also be wary of elk, especially during spring calving and fall rutting.

Cycle only on designated trails. The Canadian Parks Service publishes a list of designated trails in Alberta's and B.C.'s mountain national parks. The rest are closed to cycling for reasons that include avoiding areas heavily used by hikers and protecting fragile terrain and sensitive wildlife areas. In Kananaskis Country, most of the trails are open to cycling; some restrictions apply in Peter Lougheed Provincial Park. A Kananaskis Country brochure lists mountain biking trails.

When cycling, stay on the trail. Swinging off trails to avoid mud holes and obstructions or to take a short cut or more scenic route can easily damage sensitive vegetation. In alpine areas, this type of damage can take years to repair.

Ratings

Hard-core mountain bikers would consider the majority of trips described here fairly tame. But for the many back country enthusiasts who are new to mountain biking, these outings can provide a reasonable challenge while transporting them through some magnificent countryside. It is assumed that those embarking on these trips know at least the rudiments of riding a mountain bike. Note: These trips have been chosen as outings in their own right and not merely as a quick means of accessing hiking trails or fishing lakes, though that is often an additional benefit.

Moderate: Half-day trip on smooth road.

Intermediate: Half-day trip or longer with some rough sections but usually on a good road or trail.

Strenuous: Half-day trip or longer with lots of up and down, significant rough stretches, and perhaps some walking up and down steeper hills.

Advanced: Usually a full day's outing, with lots of rough stretches (i.e. higher risk of spills) and often steep hills to climb or descend. Some pushing a definite possibility.

Mountain Bike Check-list

Although a mountain bike can get you in and out of the mountains in a hurry, it can also leave you stranded a long way from the trailhead with either a breakdown or an injury. Thus you should carry much of the same precautionary gear you would for hiking. See the check-list at the beginning of Chapter 1 for basic gear that should be considered for mountain biking. Given that a serious breakdown 30 kilometres from your car can easily result in an unexpected overnight stay, you should also consider taking some emergency gear (such as a bivy sack) for long, difficult outings.

- Helmet—Never cycle without one.
- Bicycle bell
- Water bottle
- Cycling gloves
- Mud protectors (optional)
- Padded cycling pants or shorts (optional). Note: It's easy to get the pant leg of loose-fitting shorts caught on the seat on dismounts.
- Headlamp

Repair Kit—Potentially the most important thing you carry. Consider packing some, if not all, of the following:

- Tire pump
- Patching kit

- Spare spokes
- Spoke wrench
- Chain rivet tool and spare chain links
- Allen wrenches
- 8/9/10 mm socket
- Crescent wrench
- Freewheel remover
- Phillips and slotted screwdrivers

Note: Carrying a lot of gear in a pack can be sweaty and tiring, especially on your neck and shoulders. The weight can be distributed somewhat by carrying your tools in a small bag mounted under the front handlebars and lashing small packs to a rear carrier. Water bottles can also be secured in a holder on the front fork. The trade-off is that loading your bike with too much gear can restrict manoeuvrability.

PLATEAU MOUNTAIN

• **Distance:** 6 kilometres to the south end • **Rating:** Moderate • **Time:** 2–3 hours return • **Elevation Gain:** 400 metres (1300 feet) • **Topo Map:** 82 J/2 Fording River • **Access:** From the Highwood Junction, where Highways 40 and 541 meet, drive 26 kilometres south on the Forest Trunk Road (S.R. 940). Take a side road to the left, past a sour gas warning sign, and drive 3.9 kilometres to a locked gate.

PLATEAU MOUNTAIN IS one of the best mountain bike trips in Alberta and a fine introduction to the neglected mountains of south Kananaskis Country. The route is nearly all above tree line, offering endless views of peaks and prairie as it follows a broad ridge. This is a rare mountain biking road so smooth you can enjoy the scenery as you pedal.

The vistas are not the only compelling reason to visit Plateau Mountain. This broad tabletop remained an ice-free zone for plants and animals during the last period of glaci-

Cycling along Plateau Mountain.

ation. (Ironically, there is, at the north end of the plateau, an ice cave, now protected from further deterioration by a gate across its entrance.) The absence of glacial abrasion combined with many years of freeze-thaw action has allowed the rocks to assume interesting patterns. Today, these features are preserved in the Plateau Mountain Natural Area.

The cycling begins just below tree line, thanks to the elevation gained by driving partway up the road. The first 4 kilometres are mostly uphill on a broad, hard-packed road that soon rises above the forest. Ahead, the plateau looks like an enormous beached whale, its broad back stretching flat for several kilometres.

At 4.5 kilometres, the trail levels off somewhat at a fork. The side route to the north is thinner, rougher, and looser but still good by mountain biking standards and worth the gentle run down to an old drilling platform. Right under your wheels are delicate moss campion, their spongy green turf producing pink flowers on slender stalks in midsummer. Nearby, among the patterned rocks covered in black lichen, small spruce struggle to secure a livelihood in this exposed alpine environment.

You, too, are likely to be buffeted by the strong winds that are a constant companion in southern Alberta. But the steady breeze also provides updrafts that allow hawks to hang suspended for hours, their sharp eyes alert for day-dreaming ground squirrels. I have seen another carnivore here, the ground-hugging weasel, sliding effortlessly through the rocks at dusk.

From a rise above the drilling platform, one can make out the distant office towers of downtown Calgary to the north-east. Closer at hand, the cracked hills below creep onto rolling ranch lands.

Back at the junction, the smooth road is regained, the grade levelling off as the route heads south. The panoramas from this high plateau are capable of expanding the soul. To the west, the peaks of the High Rock Range rise to form a silhouette on the horizon. To the south, beyond three rows of ridges, one can see on a clear day all the way to Chief Mountain on the U.S. border. To the east, the crumbled rocky ridges give way in ever greener waves to the vast prairie and open skies beyond.

The only blight on this unique landscape is a nearby sour gas structure and radio tower. But it is perhaps hypocritical to decry these man-made intrusions after riding up a smooth road built to service them. At least the radio tower is powered by a small wind turbine. The sour gas extracted here contains hydrogen sulphide gas, which is extremely toxic in the rare event of a leak or blow out. If you don't mind riding past the dire warning signs, you can cycle out to the southern edge of the plateau, which overlooks the Hailstone Butte lookout and secondary road 532 far below.

The extremely ambitious can cycle east from the radio tower and then walk and ride their bikes down a ridge to join the Hailstone Butte lookout road and then the Forestry Trunk Road, making for a loop trip of nearly 40 kilometres.

Otherwise, return the way you came, a fast descent on a flawless road. But you may find yourself applying the brakes often, not for any loose rocks, but to stop and savour this marvellous landscape on the edge of the Rockies.

ODLUM POND

• **Rating:** Intermediate • **Distance:** 28 kilometres return • **Time:** 4–5 hours • **Elevation Gain:** 300 metres (1000 feet) • **Topo Map:** 82 J/7 Mount Head • **Access:** Drive 12.2 kilometres north of Highwood Junction on Highway 40 and park at the Lineham Creek picnic area on the right. From the parking lot, cycle 200 metres north on the highway and then angle left through the ditch and around a gate to gain a grassy road. Alternatively, ride less than a kilometre farther on the highway and then drop down a steep bank at a large clearing to pick up the trail. Note: This stretch of Highway 40 is closed from December 1 until June 15.

THE RIDE ALONG Odlum Creek is an enjoyable cycle through forest on a good gravel and dirt road. For excitement, there's a minor ford at the beginning of the trip. For beauty, there's the lure at the end of the trail of a lovely pond tucked beneath a big rock wall.

At the outset, the biggest challenge is to dodge the cow pies produced by cattle grazing along the ditch. Although it is a recreational area, the southern part of Kananaskis Country is a multi-use zone that allows grazing and hunting, so wear red if you're cycling in the fall.

About 1.5 kilometres from the parking lot, cyclists must ford the Highwood River, which can be quite high during spring run-off and still knee-deep in the fall. At times, there are small trees fallen across a narrowing of the river, but it would require a precarious balancing act to cross with a bike on your shoulders. So it's best to roll up your pants and make the quick dash through the chilly water. You might want to use an old pair of sneakers for the crossing and leave them for the return plunge.

Beyond the river, the dirt and grass road rises gently through a succession forest of lodgepole pine. At 3 kilometres, it reaches tiny Loomis Creek, crossed by vigorous cycling or by walking across a nearby plank. Immediately after the crossing, take the broad, flat road to the right that follows the Highwood River. The steeper, narrower trail to the left leads to Loomis Lake, a more challenging destination for another day.

As the trail continues through sun-dappled forest, keep an eye out for ripe strawberries and for ruffed grouse pecking for food alongside the road. Because grouse blend so well into their surroundings, you're more apt to hear than see them, especially if they suddenly flush with an explosion of beating wings from beneath your wheels. The male ruffed grouse performs a spectacular mating ritual, standing on a log and furiously beating his wings to produce a drumming sound that builds to a climax.

Bypass a steeper short cut to the left and continue rising

Odlum Pond.

gently through a forest of aspen, pine, and Engelmann spruce. At the crest of one steep but ridable hill, there's a brief and impressive view of a sharp mountain ridge that serves as a marker of the route ahead. You are now heading west and following Odlum Creek, hidden in the trees below. With luck, you may spot a moose browsing in a clearing.

The scars of logging are evident here, particularly at the site of an old mill crossed by the road. The clearing does, however, provide views of the thickly forested hills across the valley. The road begins to deteriorate as it drops toward Odlum Creek, a lovely brook winding through another saw-mill site.

Ignore the bridge crossing and pick up an overgrown trail along the south side of the creek. There are ridable stretches beyond, but the going is generally so rough and boggy that it's best to abandon your bicycles and walk the remaining short distance to Odlum Pond.

The shallow pond is less impressive than its backdrop, an imposing north face that forms the southern end of a line of three summits; Mount Odlum is the farthest removed. Beyond the pond, Odlum Creek cascades in a braided water-fall down the steep slope from its source above a high grove of larch. The game trails that criss-cross the rocky slopes across the way are evidence of bighorn sheep in the area.

The return trip is a fast descent that becomes increasingly enjoyable as the gradient eases, ending with a long glide through the forest and a final dash through the Highwood River.

BRYANT CREEK

• **Rating:** Intermediate • **Distance:** About 40 kilometres return • **Elevation Gain:** 150 metres (500 feet) • **Time:** About 6 hours return • **Topo Maps:** 82 J/14 Spray Lakes and 82 J/13 Mount Assiniboine • **Access:** Drive to the Mount Shark (Engadine Lodge) road off the Smith-Dorrien-Spray Trail—29 kilometres north from the Highway 40 junction or 39 kilometres south of Canmore—and head 5.4 kilometres west to the Mount Shark parking lot. Once on your bicycle, follow the Watridge Lake signs.

HOP ON A MOUNTAIN bike and suddenly the usual, long backpack into Assiniboine becomes a half-day ride encompassing one national and two provincial parks. But even if you venture no farther than the flats below Assiniboine Pass, as described here, the cycle along Bryant Creek makes for a pleasant outing on a smooth dirt road through forest and willowy meadows. A bicycle also provides hikers and fishermen with quick access to the splendid lakes and passes along the way. Be forewarned that a couple of days a week, bikers and hikers must share the valley with helicopters carrying people into Assiniboine.

Initially, the Watridge Lake trail is a gravel road passing through clear-cut blocks, which were logged prior to the establishment of Kananaskis Country in 1977. Intersecting the road at frequent intervals are grassy trails that in winter are track-set courses for cross-country ski racers. But it's hard to get lost as the route is signed every few hundred metres.

The logging scars are soon replaced by enclosed forest and the gravel by a dirt road covered in wood chips (hopefully not from the lost trees nearby). At 3.2 kilometres, a short trail to the left leads down to Watridge Lake, a popular fishing spot for cutthroat. Less than a kilometre's walk south of the lake, Karst Spring—one of the largest springs of its kind in North America—bubbles up mysteriously from the north slope of Mount Shark and cascades over mossy boulders.

Back on the main trail, the route drops steeply over a treed ridge to cross the bridged Spray River. To the left, a hiking-only trail leads up the Spray Valley to the river's source at the southern tip of Banff National Park. To the right, the Spray flows past visible tree stumps into the Spray Lakes Reservoir before escaping towards Banff.

A little farther on, a slightly rougher trail crosses Bryant Creek, a lovely, slow-flowing stream that will be your nearby companion the rest of the trip. Turn left at the Bryant Creek junction and ignore a side-trail to the left that leads to a warden's cabin. You are now in Banff National Park and gently climbing along a wide dirt trail cleared some years ago by caterpillar, when environmental sensibilities were less refined. Still, there is a feeling of being enclosed in the pine forest that crowds the trail.

Stop at Big Springs Campground (9 kilometres) and fill your bottle with the rushing spring water that descends over mossy green rocks from the fractured Cone Mountain to the right. This and the connecting peaks have periodically lost some of their rocky slopes, as evidenced by the large boulder fields the trail climbs over near the Marvel Lake turn-off.

Following this short, steep section, the route descends quickly to the Bryant Creek warden cabin, one of the older such cabins in the park, with a carved wooden Indian head over the door. Though not as frequently as they would probably like, wardens in the mountain national parks still ride on horseback, and occasionally on mountain bikes, in to these cabins, which serve as often remote outposts for the areas they patrol. The porch of this cabin provides an excellent overview of the suddenly broad valley leading to Assiniboine Pass. Many peaks are now visible, including to the southwest the glaciated Eon, which feeds nearby Marvel Lake.

Many backpackers spend the night in the nearby campground, but as only a couple of hours have passed by bicycle, there's still plenty of time for further exploration. Beyond the warden's cabin, the trail through the meadow is still good, though it gets rougher and muddier as one approaches Assiniboine Pass. At a fork in the trail, most cyclists take the better hiking trail.

Unless you're intent on pushing your bike, or hiking, up over the pass to B.C.'s Assiniboine Provincial Park, this is a good place to turn around. The return trip is considerably faster, other than the steep hill near Watridge Lake. Just before the parking lot, there's a good view over the south end of the Spray Lakes Reservoir and the surrounding peaks.

Assiniboine Provincial Park Option

As of this writing, cyclists are allowed into the park, though it's mostly a push to the top of Assiniboine Pass. Even so, it's worth the effort on a clear day to see one of the wonders of the Rockies, Mount Assiniboine (3618 metres), its pyramid-shaped summit towering over Lake Magog. Along the lake's shores is Assiniboine Lodge, built by the CPR in the 1920s and a popular ski destination for decades. Nearby, the government-run Naiset Cabins are available for a reasonable fee on a first-come, first-serve basis.

Marvel Lake and Owl Lake Hiking Options

One of the larger lakes in Banff National Park, Marvel Lake is a popular destination for hikers and fishers, though over-fishing has led to recent reductions in limits. It's a 1.1-kilometre walk from the 13-kilometre campground near the Bryant Creek Trail. Many hikers and backpackers carry on over Wonder Pass, an alternate route to Assiniboine.

The Owl Lake junction is about 2 kilometres closer to the Bryant Creek trailhead. It's a 3.5-kilometre walk to this blue-green lake. If you have time and initiative, it's worth an additional 4-kilometre hike beyond the end of Owl Lake to Marvel Pass, where a lovely little lake and splendid alpine views are the rewards of a 300-metre vertical ascent.

MOOSE MOUNTAIN FIRE LOOKOUT

• **Rating:** Intermediate • **Distance:** 12 kilometres return • **Time:** 3–4 hours • **Elevation Gain:** 470 metres (1540 feet) to the lookout • **Topo Map:** 82 J/15 Bragg Creek • **Access:** Drive 17 kilometres southwest of Bragg Creek on Highway 66. Just past the Paddy Flat's sign, turn right onto an unmarked but good gravel road and drive 7 kilometres to the trailhead, on the right.

THIS ROCKY TRAIL along a broad, windswept ridge offers cyclists stirring evidence of the sharply contrasting geography of southern Alberta. Rising above forested foothills, Moose Mountain provides commanding views of the prairies and Calgary's urban sprawl to the east and the Rocky Mountain front ranges to the immediate west. An added bonus is a fire lookout, which from the switchbacks below resembles a fairy tale castle perched high on a hill.

The good news is you can gain this view by mountain bike within two hours of leaving Calgary's city limits, making this a great evening excursion. The bad news is you'll likely have to abandon your bike before some steep switchbacks, or at least push it up. But by then, you may want to savour the surroundings on foot anyway.

The drive up the sour gas road shortens the approach considerably and cuts a few hundred metres off the ascent. Still, there's a fair amount of elevation yet to be gained, so don't expect many flat stretches.

Be forewarned that the track, while fairly wide and of only moderate difficulty, contains considerable stretches of loose rocks and boulders. A helmet, gloves, and long pants and sleeves are thus recommended. If this type of trail is not to your liking, the fire lookout road also makes a good day-hike, especially in the spring, when Moose Mountain becomes one of the first peaks to lose its snow cover.

The route is up and down in the early going, including a lengthy descent over loose rocks; remember, it's no shame to walk your bike, especially if no one's looking. The cover of pine and spruce forest briefly gives way to a flowered meadow and the first views of low mountains to the southwest.

After a short uphill grunt, the forest is left behind for

good. (Some cyclists hide their bikes in woods here and proceed on foot.) In its place is a rounded grassy ridge, an ideal place to catch your breath and marvel at the dramatic change from prairie to foothills to low mountains. With any luck, you will have chosen a calm day, as the ridge is exposed to high winds that often sweep through the foothills.

Ahead lies a series of gravelly switchbacks up a hill. From a distance, this challenge doesn't appear too daunting. But unless you're equipped with mammoth thighs, iron lungs, and superb balance, it's much more pleasant to walk than ride. Above the hill, the ridge briefly levels out again, revealing the fire lookout at the top of a steep hill. You definitely won't ride up this one, but it doesn't take long to trudge up to the summit, where the views are truly panoramic.

Return the way you came, retrieving your bike wherever you left it. The descent is fast but keep your speed under control as the loose rocks can send you for an unwelcome header over the handlebars.

VALLEY OF THE FIVE LAKES TO OLD FORT POINT

• **Rating:** Strenuous • **Distance:** 23.5 kilometres return
• **Time:** About 3-4 hours • **Topo Map:** 83 D/16 Jasper
• **Access:** From the traffic lights at the south entrance to Jasper townsite, drive 9 kilometres south on Highway 93 and park at the trailhead to Valley of the Five Lakes.

THIS IS A PLEASANT trip through a montane valley boasting a diversity of charms. Squeezed into a few kilometres are a marsh, five exquisite little lakes, grassy slopes, and several species of trees, all set amidst rolling hills. The observant can look for moose, loons, blue heron, beaver, ruffed grouse, and a profusion of wild flowers, including the lovely calypso orchid. If you don't mind some rough sections and undulating riding throughout, this is one of the best ways to spend half a day in the Jasper area.

Trail traversing above one of the five small lakes, Valley of the Five Lakes.

The trail begins smoothly enough as it passes through lodgepole pine and aspen forest before descending to a boardwalk across a slough fed by Wabasso Creek. This reedy environment is home to great blue herons, beavers, and a variety of songbirds. Ignore a bisecting trail and climb a short hill to a ridge above the slough. Look back and admire the snowy north face of Mount Edith Cavell, the highest (3363 metres) and most striking peak in the immediate Jasper vicinity.

From this hill, follow the trail to the right, which leads to the fourth and fifth lakes, just over 2 kilometres from the trailhead. Take care on the short but rocky descent to the lakes, walking the bike if necessary. Here one can either swing to the right around the end of the fifth lake or carry the bike across a few rocks between the fourth and fifth lakes.

Beyond, the dirt trail traversing above the east side of the lakes is the most scenic part of the trip. The view south from the open, grassy slopes encompasses the lakes below and the broad Athabasca Valley beyond as far as Mount Kerkeslin. These five bodies of water, rimmed in light green, are more the size of ponds than lakes. Only the first lake, encircled in trees, extends for any distance below the trail.

At several spots along the lakes, there are fire pits, often thoughtfully stocked with stacks of cut firewood. It's a perfect invitation for those wishing to spend a pleasant evening by the lakes, listening for loons and waiting for the moon to rise.

Beyond the lakes, keep an eye out for a trail to the right leading up a hillside of fir and aspen. If you miss the junction, you'll end up following a thin trail along a creek that ends up as a bushwhack through willows.

The remaining 7 kilometres to Old Fort Point pass through one of the area's larger aspen forests, which turns a lovely shade of yellow in fall. The trail is broad but rarely flat, with lots of short up-and-down sections that occasionally require dismounting and pushing. Now and then, smooth, sandy, stretches appear, allowing one to safely build up a head of steam. Remember to periodically yell out or ring your bell to avoid surprise encounters at high speed with bears that might be patrolling the valley.

The trail dips to cross Tekarra Creek and then continues its undulating course. A few kilometres from the end, there's a thin side-trail to the left that traverses along a grassy hillside, offering extensive views over the forest. Rather than descend a steep hillside beyond, backtrack to the main trail.

Just ahead, there is a junction with trails marked 1 and 1A. Follow the latter, to the right, and ease your way down a steep hill that may require walking. Take heart. The hilly terrain is now behind you, and it's a fast cruise on a smooth sandy road to Old Fort Point. I once saw a marten scampering along this road ahead of me, taking refuge up a tree as I overtook it.

At Old Fort Point, you may wish to hide your bike in the bushes and take the short hike up to the point, an exposed knoll that provides one of the best views of the landscape surrounding Jasper. Old Fort Point is located near the site of Henry House, built in 1811 to support the fur brigades crossing the Rocky Mountains.

From Old Fort Point, cross the bridge over the Athabasca River, turn left on Highway 93A and left again on Highway 93, which is followed back to the parking lot, a return of nearly 11 kilometres.

MOUNT RUNDLE LOOP

• **Rating:** Advanced • **Distance:** 31 kilometres • **Elevation Gain:** None • **Time:** 5–6 hours • **Topo Maps:** 82 O/3 Canmore and 82 O/4 Banff • **Access:** Drive 9 kilometres south of Canmore on the Smith-Dorrien-Spray Trail to the top of Whiteman Gap. Pull over at the top of the steep hill for a marvellous view of the Bow River corridor and the rampant development of Canmore at your feet. The Goat Creek trailhead is in a large parking lot on the west side of the road, just past a deep reservoir pond. If you have another vehicle, leave it at the Canmore Nordic Centre closer to town. Otherwise, you'll have a steep, 5-kilometre ride up a busy gravel road to end your trip.

THE MOUNT RUNDLE Loop is a Jekyll and Hyde circumnavigation of one of the most recognizable peaks in the Rockies. The first half is a delightful downhill cruise on dirt and gravel roads to the Banff Springs Hotel. The return trip towards Canmore is a spine-jarring roller-coaster ride over roots and rocks alongside the Bow River. Those wishing a calmer trip can return to Canmore along the Trans-Canada Highway. Chiropractics aside, this is a fine tour of human and geological history.

The 17-kilometre stretch from Whiteman Gap to Banff is justifiably one of the most popular mountain bike trips in Alberta, so expect lots of company on a warm summer's day. The old logging and fire roads one follows are mostly smooth, as are the ramped bridge crossings of side streams and rivers. Best of all, the lofty start at Whiteman Gap ensures the ride to Banff is almost entirely downhill on a pleasant grade, quite a switch from the uphill grunts and steep descents of most mountain bike trips. You can thus easily reach the Banff Springs Hotel in less than two hours, arriving for afternoon tea with scarcely a drop of perspiration on your brow.

From the Whiteman Gap parking lot, a dirt and gravel logging road descends northwest and follows Goat Creek through open forest that offers glimpses of Mount Rundle. About 1 kilometre from the trailhead, you leave Kananaskis Country and enter Banff National Park. Incidentally, the latter's eastern boundaries extended farther east until they were retracted in 1930, allowing development to proceed along the Smith-Dorrien valley.

It's easy to pick up speed along the straightaways so keep an eye out for a sharp left-hand turn and steep descent to a crossing of Goat Creek. A little farther on, the road crosses the Spray River, a good place to gaze at Mount Rundle and the Goat Range and contemplate the river's source at the distant south end of Banff National Park.

Just beyond, the Goat Creek trail merges with the Spray River Fire Road, a high-grade gravel road built to provide park officials with access to the southern part of the park. Turn right and keep cruising towards Banff. A picnic grounds at a riverside clearing offers the option of crossing Four Mile Bridge and following a narrower track alongside the Spray. Otherwise, continue on the fire road. With little effort, you are soon high above the river and looking north to the folded strata of Cascade Mountain, a Banff landmark.

The road enters a cool forest, a good place to slow down and enjoy the quiet of these mossy woods. About 1 kilometre from the end of the road, it's worth detouring down a side-trail to a wooden bridge crossing the Spray River. An abandoned quarry nearby produced rocks used in the construction of such buildings as the Banff Springs Hotel, which coincidentally stands majestically in view downstream.

The Banff Springs was built as a 250-room palace by the Canadian Pacific Railway to lure tourists to the mountains by rail. The largest hotel in the world when completed in 1888, the building has undergone a number of additions and renovations in the ensuing century. It remains the most recognized landmark in Banff, though its latest expansion is representative of the never-ending commercial development in the town of Banff. When you reach the hotel, lock your bike, stroll through the stone hallways, and enjoy a refreshment in the lounge overlooking Bow Falls.

You may need a stiff drink to loosen your chassis for the rough ride ahead. The return trip begins gently enough, following a paved road alongside the velvety fairways of the Banff Springs Golf Course. A helmet may come in handy as protection from wayward shots. About 3.7 kilometres from the bridge below the hotel, there is an unmarked and easily missed shelter, which marks the start of the Rundle Riverside Trail to Canmore.

Here the roller-coaster ride begins. The narrow trail is full of roots and rocks and goes constantly up and down. The biggest danger is not a high-speed tumble but catching a pedal on one of the many projections, so remove any toe clips before embarking. Because there is only one track and many blind corners, ring your bike bell often to avoid nasty surprises. Still, the trail is mostly ridable and if you can persevere through the first couple of kilometres, the going gets progressively easier (or maybe you just get used to it).

This section is not without its charms, especially when you dismount. The Bow River winds peacefully nearby and early stretches of emerald forest are quite enchanting. Several avalanche crossings offer good views of the broad Bow Valley. The cliffs above you are part of the northeast face of Mount Rundle (2949 metres), which stretches for some 20 kilometres from Banff to Canmore.

Rundle is actually a series of connected peaks, the highest of which is the third south from Banff. The views of Rundle change dramatically depending on the perspective. As seen from west of Banff, the angled southwest slopes rise in a single plane towards the summit ridge. By contrast, the northeast face drops sharply away. Seen in profile, this face clearly shows its layers—limestone, in the form of steep cliffs at the top and bottom, and slopes of eroded shale in between. Mount Rundle is named after Robert Rundle, a Methodist missionary who worked among the Stoney Indians near Banff in the late 1840s.

Eventually, the forest obscures all views, although the overhead canopy opens up as you approach Canmore Nordic Centre. After 8 kilometres, the boundary of Kananaskis Country is reached and is followed by the Banff Trail, a 6-kilometre stretch of smooth gravel road. This bisects many of the developed cross-country ski trails that extend from Canmore Nordic Centre, including those used during the 1988 Winter Olympics.

These trails pass not far from Georgetown, where a coal mine flourished in the years before World War I. When mining shifted to nearby seams, the miners skidded their houses down on logs to the western edge of Canmore. The Canmore Mine closed in 1979.

Just beyond the biathlon shooting range is the final descent into the stadium. If no one is watching, you can raise arms and pretend you're being greeted as the runaway winner of the 50-kilometre Olympic ski race. In reality, you're more likely just relieved to be finished.

ELBOW LOOP

• **Rating:** Advanced • **Distance:** 42 kilometres • **Time:** 5–8 hours • **Elevation Gain:** 640 metres (2100 feet) • **Topo Maps:** 82 J/10 Mount Rae and 82 J/15 Bragg Creek • **Access:** From Bragg Creek, drive 32 kilometres southwest on Highway 66 to its terminus at Little Elbow Recreation Area. Cycle to the west end of the campground and past a gate to reach the Little Elbow Trail, on the north side of the river.

THIS GRAND TOUR through the Front Ranges of Kananaskis Country is one of the best and most varied mountain bike trips in Alberta. Not for the timid, it demands strong legs, perseverance, and good downhill riding skills. But the industrious are amply rewarded with sublime alpine meadows, high vistas, an open hillside traverse, and all the adventure one could want in a full day of cycling. A mountain bike is the ideal way to see this wild country, the wheels eating up the distance on old four-wheel-drive roads that would take hours to hike. This makes a good outing in June, when snow still clings to higher trails elsewhere, or in late September, when the larch have turned to orange.

The Elbow Loop is a circumnavigation of Banded Peak and Mounts Glasgow and Cornwall, three of the more substantial peaks in the eastern ranges of Kananaskis Country. They form the bulk around which flow two rivers, the Elbow and Little Elbow. The first half of the trip traces the Little Elbow drainage to its lofty source near Tombstone Lakes. Only about 3 kilometres beyond lies the Elbow, which is followed for nearly 20 kilometres before it joins the Little Elbow en route for Bragg Creek and then Calgary.

From the trailhead, the slightly rough road passes for 12 kilometres through rolling terrain, the little hills along the way but a warm-up for the grunt ahead. Not far beyond the campground, a hiking trail to the right leads to Nihahi Ridge, a superb ridge walk with views to the west of the Opal Range. Two kilometres farther up the road, a northbound trail follows Nihahi Creek past a fascinating small canyon of water-polished rocks.

Shortly thereafter, the road crosses a bridge to the south side of the Little Elbow and flattens out as it passes through mixed forest and meadow. Rising above the forested valley to the north is the flat-topped bulk of Mount Romulus, named for one of the twin brothers who founded Rome. The lower Mount Remus is just to the east.

At 12 kilometres, just past the Mount Romulus campground, a junction is reached. A clearing provides views up two drainages, the Little Elbow's west and north forks, which merge nearby before entering the river. Your mission, however, is to head south and follow the Little Elbow to its source, and a lofty source it is, rising some 400 metres above this valley.

For the next 8 kilometres, you might find yourself cursing the joys of mountain biking as you pedal endlessly uphill in low gear. The only relief for paining thighs is to walk your bike across rocky outwashes and up some of the steeper hills. But persistence is amply rewarded by one of the finest stretches of mountain biking you'll find in the Rockies, plus the realization that nearly all the uphill riding is behind you.

The first attraction, as the grade eases, is a lovely willow and spruce meadow, the greenery accentuated by a thin, clear stream curving along the road. Just before Little Elbow Pass, a short hiking trail leads to Tombstone Lakes, two small bodies of water guarded by the massive limestone walls of Tombstone Mountain.

The pass is bisected by one of the most extensive forests of alpine larch in the Rockies, making this a good fall destination, when the deciduous needles have turned to orange. From this lofty perch, there is a panoramic view of ridges, rock faces, and, to the south, the Misty Range and its highest peak, Mount Rae. The broad meadows, full of summer flowers, are a good place to lunch and savour the alpine splendour.

Once the bicycle is remounted, the preciously gained elevation is lost at a dramatic rate. The rocky road drops steeply for a couple of kilometres, testing your brakes and downhill technique. The practice of clenching the back of the seat between the thighs will lower your centre of gravity and ease the feeling of teetering over the handlebars.

The plunge continues into forest, the scenery blurring by, though the view above the trees is compelling if you can glance up long enough. It's better to dismount at viewpoints and enjoy the distant, velvety ridges as well as the paintbrush and glacier lilies growing along the dirt road.

Before you reach the bottom of this long hill, keep a sharp lookout for a narrower trail, which is taken to the left. This dirt track undulates like a roller-coaster as it climbs to a high bench, offering the first views of the Elbow River and the stratified layers of Banded Peak.

The trail takes a spectacular line as it traverses a grassy hillside high above the Elbow. Keep your eye on this slender path to avoid careening down the slope. Beyond the hillside, there are a few short descents around boulders that will test your nerve and skill.

The trail soon joins a wider road, featuring several more kilometres of up-and-down terrain, washouts, and small creeks to cross plus several short but steep descents to navigate. There are still a dozen kilometres to go, but just when you think this tortuous route will go on forever, the Elbow River is crossed on a bridge and a broad road gained.

This is the smoothest track you've been on all day and, if you're blessed with a tail wind, the kilometres start to fly by as you shift into high gear. The road soon emerges from the forest and enters a broad valley, down which the Elbow flows in braided channels. While it's no torrent, the Elbow does provide spring thrills for white-water canoeists and kayakers farther downstream. It also supplies nearly half of Calgary's drinking water.

In spring, you get a chance to test these waters, albeit in a mild way, as a run-off channel briefly joins the road. It's usually shallow enough to easily ride through, if you keep the pedals moving. After a short stretch through forest, the Little Elbow is again reached. Rather than attempt a ford, take a short detour to the left and cross on a suspension bridge to reach the trailhead.

Cyclist nearing Highwood Pass.

CHAPTER FIVE

Road Cycle Trips

Introduction

*A*lberta is blessed not only with magnificent scenery but also with excellent roads from which to enjoy it. Most of the province's paved highways are in good condition—potholes are rare—and the shoulders are more generous than in most provinces or states. Indeed, some of the best roads are the paved secondary highways that few people explore.

One of the best ways to travel southern and western Alberta's roads is by bicycle. The cyclist gains a much different perspective of the landscape than the speeding motorist, who watches the scenery blur by through the filter of a windshield. On a bicycle, mountains move by more slowly, grazing elk are almost within reach, and the sun, wind, and rain can be experienced directly. The slower pace also encourages cyclists to pull over and savour the splendour or roll down to a riverside for a picnic lunch.

Safety

The biggest concern with road cycling is safety. Cyclists are pretty much at the mercy of vehicles, which can stray onto the shoulder or kick up rocks as they pass. The best strategy is to minimize the risk of accidents.

First, steer clear of roads that are narrow, busy, and have no shoulders. Some narrow roads, such as the Bow Valley Parkway near Banff, can be a joy to ride because they are lightly travelled, have few sharp corners, and are much more intimate than major thoroughfares. But add a few thousand cars and some sharp bends, and a narrow road becomes a cycling hazard.

Second, drive defensively. Riding two or three abreast may stimulate conversation but will greatly increase one's exposure to passing vehicles, even on wide shoulders. Generally, stay well over onto the shoulder. A side mirror attached to the handlebars or helmet will allow you to spot approaching traffic. The alternative of making shoulder checks can cause one's bicycle to veer unexpectedly into a lane of traffic or perhaps the ditch.

Third, make yourself visible. Many cyclists have taken to wearing bright orange and reflective clothing. Another strategy is to attach to bicycles reflective triangles or thin poles topped by orange flags. If you happen to be cycling in low light or in the dark, have a good headlamp. A newer innovation is a pulsing red rear light, which can make cyclists visible from up to 700 metres away.

Ratings

The road cycling trips in this chapter range from a short ride on a paved cycling path to a major highway traverse through the Canadian Rockies. There are a few long, steep climbs and a couple pretty much on the level. Most of these outings are pleasant day-trips.

Almost anyone able to cycle can manage most of the road trips described in this chapter. A few of the longer and hillier trips require a reasonable level of fitness. The grand traverse from Jasper to Banff also demands a certain amount of stamina, as well as a talent for logistics. Other than that, the ability to pedal in a straight line for several hours and enjoy superb scenery are the major prerequisites.

Moderate: A trip of less than 30 kilometres with minor hilly sections and little or no overall elevation gain.

Strenuous: A trip of some 40 kilometres or longer with considerable elevation gain or numerous hilly sections.

Advanced: A multi-day trip over several hundred kilometres with considerable elevation gains and losses along the way. Requires carrying more gear and arranging accommodation.

Road Cycling Check-list

The good thing about road cycling is that, unlike mountain biking, you're never far from help, assuming you can catch a ride in the event of a breakdown. Still, it's best to be self-sufficient and carry an adequate amount of food, water, clothing, and repair gear. Many of the items on the list are optional, intended to make cycling more comfortable and sometimes safer.

- Touring bike or mountain bike—If you do a lot of road touring on a mountain bike, consider replacing knobby tires with a smoother tread.
- Toe clips
- Tire pump
- One or two water bottles attached to the frame
- Rear carrier
- Small bag attached to front handlebar or under the seat—Good for carrying repair kits, maps, etc.
- Panniers—For carrying loads on longer trips
- Bike lock—Handy if you plan a side-hike or have to abandon a crippled bicycle
- Side mirror
- Cycle computer (optional)—These high-tech devices

contain a clock, stopwatch, odometer, tripmeter, and provide read-outs on speed and, in some cases, average speed.

- Lights—Headlight and pulsing rear light
- Repair kit and spare parts—See mountain bike check-list in Chapter 4
- Helmet—Always wear one
- Padded, fingerless cycling gloves
- Padded lycra cycling shorts—You'll notice the difference on longer rides
- Bright or reflective clothing
- Weatherproof jacket and pants
- Overnight gear—See backpacking check-list in Chapter 2. Many cyclists pack the lightest camping gear possible.

KANANAKSIS LAKES

• **Rating:** Moderate • **Distance:** 29 kilometres return • **Time:** 3–4 hours return • **Elevation Gain:** Minimal • **Access:** From the Highway 40 junction with the Kananaskis Lakes Trail, drive 3.6 kilometres south on the latter to the Kananaskis Visitor Centre parking lot, where the paved cycling trail begins.

AT LAST, CIVILIZED cycling on a paved path. No congestion of bumpy city pathways or the ingestion of car fumes here. Just wide, perfectly smooth asphalt rolling through an emerald forest of lodgepole pine with glimpses of striking mountains. The cycling trails above the Kananaskis Lakes make for a fine family outing or a chance to while away a few pleasant hours.

Actually, this pathway is divided into three short sections of about 5 kilometres each, with numerous crossings of the Kananaskis Lakes Trail. Even cycling back on this no-shoulder

The Lakeside trail descending into lodgepole pine forest, with Mount Sarrail in the background.

vehicular road can be an enjoyable ride through forest if traffic is light. But it's worth going the distance and making half a day of it. Incidentally, these cycling paths are in winter popular cross-country ski trails, which receive relatively high amounts of snowfall because of their proximity to the continental divide.

The first section is a 4.8-kilometre ride from the Kananaskis Visitor Centre to Elkwood Campground. This stretch of pavement is aptly named Lodgepole for the profusion of pines that line the way. Indeed, the whole route is a parade through lodgepole pines, which have flourished in the aftermath of fires that have swept through the valley. The heat of such fires causes pine cones to open, their heat-resistant seeds gaining a quick toe-hold in the blackened soil. Lodgepoles eventually give way to a climax forest of spruce and fir. The straightness of lodgepole trunks, as the name indicates, makes them ideal for tipi poles.

From the visitor centre, the trail swings by a campground and then parallels Lower Kananaskis Lake, remaining in forest except for a brief interlude beneath a power line. Just before Elkwood Campground, there's a short side-trail leading right and down to William Watson Lodge, a lovely collection of log buildings, built for the disabled, with a panoramic view across the lake to Mount Indefatigable.

The second section of the trail, called Wheeler, extends for 4.6 kilometres from Elkwood to Boulton Creek. The highlight is following a ridge line high above a small valley. It's worth stopping at one of the lofty clearings here to enjoy the view of peaks across the lake. At the end of the Wheeler trail, one can buy lunch at the Boulton Creek Trading Post or head down to a picnic site along the Lower Kananaskis Lake.

The third section, Lakeside, covers 5 kilometres from Boulton Creek to Mount Sarail campground. Of the three trails, it is the most scenic and undulating, the short, steep hills forcing cyclists to briefly shift into low gear. The pavement detours through campgrounds and follows the Lower

Kananaskis Lake. At low water, the lake's upper shore line is exposed, revealing the stumps of trees cut some years ago when an upstream dam was built.

The bicycle path ends at the Mount Sarrail Campground, but it's worth carrying on another couple of kilometres on the paved vehicular road to the North Interlakes parking lot. Here one can walk onto the narrow earth dam between the Lower and Upper Kananaskis lakes and admire the view across the latter to Mounts Sarrail and the glaciated Lyautey.

Those equipped with a mountain bike can extend the trip by cycling around the north shore trail of Upper Kananaskis Lake for 3.8 kilometres to Point Campground. Others may choose to lock their bikes and take one of the area's several short walks or a longer hike. (See Mount Indefatigable hike, page 26.)

Return the same way or follow the Kananaskis Lakes Trail back to the Visitor Centre.

BOW VALLEY PARKWAY

• **Rating:** Moderate • **Distance:** 24.2 kilometres one way • **Time:** 2–3 hours one way • **Access:** From the Banff townsite west interchange, drive 30 kilometres west on the Trans-Canada Highway and turn right at the Castle Junction interchange. Drive 1 kilometre to the intersection with the Bow Valley Parkway (1A Highway) and park nearby. Leave a second vehicle near the eastern terminus of the Parkway at the Fireside picnic area, 6 kilometres west of Banff. The alternative is to cycle back the same way. • **Note:** This trip can be tackled from either end but a Castle Junction start ensures a slightly downhill ride and usually the wind at one's back.

THE BOW VALLEY Parkway, or the 1A Highway, is one of the most delightful paved roads to cycle in the Canadian Rockies. Built in 1920 as the original highway between Banff and Lake Louise, the parkway has become a quiet backwater to its congested replacement, the Trans-Canada Highway. The thin shoulder is a small price to pay for the relative quiet and intimacy of this ride through a dry montane valley. Wildlife is plentiful, especially at dusk, and there are numerous viewpoints from which to admire the diversity of meadows, marshes, and mountains. This trip covers the parkway's southwestern half, from Castle Junction almost to Banff.

In contrast to the Trans-Canada's no-nonsense line, the Bow Valley Parkway more closely follows the lay of the land. Still, the gentle grades make it an easy road to cycle at whatever speed you desire. Although traffic is light and the speed limit restricted to 60 kilometres per hour, a helmet with a side mirror is a good safety precaution given the road's narrow width. It's also a good idea to pack a lunch to enjoy at one of several roadside picnic spots. Indeed, you may wish to make this a full day-trip by taking an interpretive hike or two along the way.

About 1 kilometre beyond the start at Castle Junction, a large clearing on the right is passed. This grassy meadow was in 1883 the boom town of Silver City, a collection of 175 buildings housing 2000 people seeking their fortunes from silver and copper. Two years later, the dreams and the city were abandoned.

Long before any white men set covetous eyes on these lands, the Bow Valley was an important passageway for Indians. Protected archaeological sites along the corridor indicate a human presence some 10,000 years ago.

This stretch of road also provides excellent views of the surrounding mountains. To the east is the long south ridge of Mount Ishbel, a magnificent example of the sawtoothed limestone peaks found in the Front Ranges of the Canadian Rockies. A short distance to the north, and a couple of hundred million geological years removed, is the aptly-named Castle Mountain, a landmark of the Main Ranges. For awhile it was called Mount Eisenhower, but it never resembled Ike's profile. Across the broad Bow Valley is Pilot

Mountain which, appropriately, can be viewed from far up the valley.

At 4 kilometres, the willowy expanse of Moose Meadows is passed. It provides summer lodgings for blackbirds, flycatchers, and other songbirds. With luck, you might spot an elusive grey wolf loping through the meadows. An almost mandatory stop, 2.5 kilometres farther, is Johnston Canyon, where a self-interpretive walkway leads up the heart of this narrow defile to a stunning sequence of waterfalls, boiling waters, and brilliantly coloured rocks. Even the hordes of camera-toting tourists cannot detract from its natural splendour.

Back in the saddle, riders reach a split in the road at 8 kilometres. The eastbound fork rises along the edge of the Hillsdale slide, where thousands of years ago water-soaked rocks from retreating glaciers slid onto the valley floor. At a roadside pull-out here, a short trail leads down through forest to Pilot Pond. The tremendous carving action of these glaciers is evident from a nearby viewpoint that overlooks the U-shaped Bow Valley.

The Sawback picnic area is a good place to eat lunch and admire the jagged mountain range of the same name. Elk, too, like to browse here, gathering in winter to munch on shrubby branches and aspen bark. The stretch of road ahead, through the luminous aspen poplar forest, is also a favourite haunt of deer, bighorn sheep, and coyotes, animals best seen in early morning or evening.

Another fine lunch spot is the Muleshoe picnic site (18.5 kilometres), which offers views of two interesting phenomena. High up on Mount Cory to the east is the famous Hole-in-the-Wall, created when the rock was dissolved by meltwaters of an ancient glacier that covered the valley to this lofty height. The passage beyond the entrance was later blocked by debris. To the west below the picnic site is Muleshoe Lake, an abandoned channel of the nearby Bow River that now serves as a stopover for waterfowl, including harlequin ducks. Another nearby wetland is the

Backswamp, a rare mountain bog that harbours orchids and moose.

After a final glimpse above the forest to the famous tilted slopes of Mount Rundle, it's only 2 more kilometres to the eastern end of the Bow Valley Parkway. A side-road near its terminus leads to the Fireside picnic area, where sweaty backs and brows can be rinsed in a chilly stream.

HIGHWOOD PASS

• **Rating:** Strenuous • **Distance:** 34 kilometres return • **Time:** About 4 hours • **Elevation Gain:** 500 metres (1650 feet) • **Access:** From the Trans-Canada Highway, drive 50.5 kilometres south on Highway 40 to its junction with the Kananaskis Lakes Trail. Park alongside the road, which is barricaded from December 1 to June 15, or in the nearby King Creek lot.

LIKE ASPARAGUS SEASON, the prime time to cycle over Highwood Pass is short-lived. It exists in the few weeks prior to June 15, when the snows have melted off Canada's highest paved highway and this stretch of road remains closed to vehicular traffic. The closure is to protect herds of bighorn sheep that winter near the pass. But by June, cyclists can safely take advantage of the closure and have this beautiful paved roadway to themselves. Just keep a respectful distance from any sheep you might see.

While the route can be enjoyably cycled throughout the summer and fall, late spring is the only time you can wander brazenly across the shoulder and be king of the road instead of road kill. Be sure to get an early start, as this rite of spring has become a popular weekend outing.

This trip is a good spring tune up for the thighs, which will be burning as they churn up a hill that climbs steadily to a lofty height of 2206 metres (7237 feet). Where else can you step off a paved road and immediately be amongst subalpine larch and flowers? Along the way, you'll be flanked by some of the most striking peaks in Kananaskis Country.

The geological tour begins almost immediately upon embarking. Along the left side of the road are ripple marks in the rock caused at least 100 million years ago by waves or running water in an ancient coastline environment. These are the same marks, in a fossilized form, as those left by a stream washing over a sandy shore.

As the road rises, there are superb views of the dramatic folding and faulting of the grey limestone peaks of the Front Ranges. From the parking area at King Creek, the long jagged ridge of Mount Wintour follows the left side of the highway for nearly 5 kilometres. An even more striking example of the severe weathering of these limestone peaks can be seen by looking left to Elpoca Mountain from near the Elbow Lake trailhead. In contrast to the sharp rise of the Opal Range to your left, lovely Pocaterra Creek flows along the other side of the highway through a much leveller and forested valley.

At 5 kilometres, the Valleyview Trail loops off the highway and runs for several kilometres along a higher, parallel bench. If the snows are gone, this road (originally part of Highway 40) offers excellent views across the valley to Kananaskis Lakes.

At 12 kilometres, the Elbow Lake junction is reached. The lake and the pass beyond are just over a kilometre up the trail, a pleasant place to hike, mountain bike, or camp in the summer or fall. Above the lake, the small glacier on the north face of Mount Rae is the principal source of the Elbow River, which provides Calgary with nearly half its drinking water.

From the junction, the highway begins a steeper and unrelenting climb that will have cyclists shifting into low gear. Five kilometres later, the heavy breathing finally ends and Highwood Pass is crested.

This is a spectacular subalpine environment, with extensive views in either direction, although the often howling winds may deter an extended stay. On the left, the splendid peaks of the Misty Range extend south in a line flanking the descending highway. To the immediate right is the folded, unnamed peak that from this perspective is clawed by avalanche chutes. Beside the road, the willowy Highwood meadows are filled in late spring with thousands of yellow alpine buttercups emerging in the wake of the melting snow cover.

A nearby boardwalk leads through the meadows past sinkholes and spruce trees, some several hundred years old. Across the road are two interpretive walks. The nearest, and longest, is Ptarmigan Cirque, a trail rising steeply through ancient forest into the meadows below Mount Rae, at 3218 metres the highest peak along Highway 40. To the north is a short walk through a rock glacier, so called because the jumbled boulders move in a similar manner to an advancing glacier. All of these walks are best left to a summer or fall visit. In fact, if you're here in late spring, it's best not to venture far off the road so as to not disturb any mountain sheep that may be encountered.

The return descent is fast and constant, even on lower stretches that appeared level on the approach. A distance that took perhaps three hours to ascend can now be descended in less than half an hour. Although the road is immaculately smooth and evenly graded, a tumble here would be disastrous, so check your speed by braking periodically, especially on steeper hills. It goes without saying that a snugly-fitting helmet, gloves, long sleeves, and long pants should be worn.

There are two options to the route described above. Instead of returning the same way, continue over the pass and descend to the road closure (until June 15) at the junction of Highways 40 and 541, some 37 kilometres beyond the pass. If the road is closed, this option involves the lengthy process of driving a pick-up vehicle south of Calgary and west of Longview. The problem can be overcome by starting a group of cyclists at either end and exchanging car keys as they pass. The other alternative is to cycle all the way from King's Creek to the junction and back (110 kilometres), resulting in a very long day in which the pass must twice be ascended. Mind you, in June there's enough daylight to satisfy this masochism.

PINCHER CREEK CIRCUIT

• **Rating:** Strenuous • **Distance:** 61 kilometres • **Time:** 5–6 hours • **Access:** From its junction with Highway 22, drive 7 kilometres west on Highway 3 (the Crowsnest Highway) to its junction with Highway 507 South. • **Note:** The trip could also start in Pincher Creek or be followed in the opposite, clockwise, direction.

THIS TRIP LOOPS through the magnificent rolling countryside of southwest Alberta, one of the province's overlooked jewels. The windswept foothills near Pincher Creek provide a dramatic foreground to the Rocky Mountains, which frame the long, low Crowsnest Pass. It is a land of sweeping vistas,

Crowsnest River near Highway 3.

gnarled trees, and meandering trout streams. If one was to take up ranching, this would be the place to buy land.

Yet there are few cyclists, or even tourists, travelling these excellent secondary highways. So while others are speeding to nearby Waterton Lakes National Park or the historic sites of Crowsnest Pass, you can enjoy this foothills splendour in relative solitude.

Throughout the trip, the roads are smoothly paved and have fairly generous shoulders, other than one section where the traffic is usually light. But be prepared for some strenuous cycling. For the first half, there is scarcely a flat spot as the road follows a roller-coaster ride through the foothills. As well, the wind is customarily strong as it blows east through Crowsnest Pass. Fortunately, one can stop for a breather almost anywhere along the way and be assured of a fine view.

From the Highway 3 junction, Highway 507 passes Lee Lake, crosses the Crowsnest River, and then commences a serpentine course south through the hills. Unlike the wind-lashed landscape closer to Crowsnest Pass, the hills here are covered in dense stands of aspen, fir, and spruce that harbour deer and other wildlife. The road climbs steadily to reach a hilltop, at 7 kilometres, that provides a commanding view over ranch lands and distant foothills.

After passing through a beautiful pine forest, the highway drops sharply at 10 kilometres to a bridge crossing the Castle River. Notice the trees clinging perilously to the steep banks. The Castle and Crowsnest rivers have lost their downstream reaches to the backwaters created by a recent dam built near their confluences with the Oldman River. But here they are still beautiful foothills streams that attract trout fishermen and experienced canoeists.

Beyond the Crowsnest, the highway climbs past a rodeo grounds and drops yet again. The view has now shifted east towards the prairie. At 14.4 kilometres, turn left onto 507 East, where the shoulder narrows. Before doing so, it's worth a

1-kilometre detour to the hamlet of Beaver Mines, a lovely spot where a number of cottages and cabins have recently risen. The store is a good place to pick up snacks and stock up on fishing flies and advice.

About 1 kilometre east on 507, a one-room brick school-house is passed. The trees are thinner and the views more expansive as one enters true foothills ranching country. A few kilometres down the road, dudes can turn south, head to Gladstone Ranch, and try their hands at riding horses into the magnificent foothills.

At about 19 kilometres, the highway drops again and passes through a fertile valley containing clusters of build-ings. Three kilometres farther, another highway leads south to Beauvais Lake Provincial Park, one of the finest places to camp in southwest Alberta.

As the road gets closer to Pincher Creek, the views open up to the north, revealing the verdant foothills valley along Highway 22. This is a good opportunity to look back west over the naked hills to the U-shaped Crowsnest Pass. Then, suddenly and startlingly, the road crests onto high prairie that is flat save for a few knobbly hills to the south.

The town of Pincher Creek was named for a pair of pincers, used to trim horse hooves, found here in the 1860s. Today, it services the farming and ranching community. If you're riding through during the annual rodeo, check out the cowboy poetry readings.

From Pincher Creek, it's a short ride north to Highway 3 and the 25-kilometre return to the car. The shoulder on the Crowsnest Highway is nearly 2 metres wide, which pro-vides some insulation from the steady stream of summer traffic. But there's no protection if the wind is howling out of the west, unless you've strategically placed a pick-up vehi-cle nearby. If you don't like traffic and don't mind gravel, there is a side-road to the north, accessible from near Cowley, that follows the lovely bends of the Crowsnest River.

Otherwise, proceed on Highway 3, enjoying the continu-

ous views of the approaching foothills, pass, and the blocky
Crowsnest Mountain. I often stop at the roadside store in
Lundbreck for a soft ice-cream cone. Just before the Highway 22 junction, take the short loop road south to Lundbreck
Falls, where the Crowsnest River tumbles some 12 metres
over a rocky ledge. At times, you can see small fish leaping
in the foaming water at the foot of the falls. It's a good place
to soak your feet in the shallow river and have a snack before
the final stretch.

Back on Highway 3, it's only a few more kilometres to complete the loop. If you have time, it's well worth driving the
short distance through the municipality of Crowsnest Pass,
a conglomeration of several small mining towns. This is a
historic area, where the Canadian Pacific Railway built a
branch line in 1898 to exploit the rich coal seams.

The blasting for coal may have contributed to the famous
Frank Slide in 1903, when 82 million tonnes of limestone
slid from the summit of Turtle Mountain, burying a section
of the town of Frank and killing some seventy people. The
jumbled rocks today extend beyond the highway and part
way up the other side of the valley to the Frank Slide
Interpretive Centre, which tells the area's story well. It's also
worth visiting the nearby Leitch Collieries, a once sophisti-
cated coal mining and coking operation, the ruins of which
are now a provincial historic site.

JASPER TO BANFF

• **Rating:** Long and Strenuous • **Distance:** 287 kilometres
• **Time:** 3–5 days • **Elevation Gain:** 330 metres (1080 feet)
overall, with considerable elevation gains and losses along
the way • **Access:** Drive to Jasper, or transport your bicycle
there by bus or, from Edmonton, by train. Using public transportation eliminates the need to return to Jasper to pick up
your vehicle. • **Note:** This trip can also be started from Banff.

Cycling on the Icefields Parkway near Bow Summit.

THE ROAD FROM Jasper to Banff is one of the great mountain tours of the world. It follows the headwaters of three major river systems, crosses two high passes, bypasses turquoise lakes and a roadside glacier, and traverses beneath some of the highest and most elegant mountains in the Canadian Rockies. En route, you might see black and grizzly bears, mountain goats, moose, and, almost assuredly, bighorn sheep and elk. Not surprisingly, this classic route attracts cyclists from around the world.

This is no wilderness trip, as cyclists share the magnificent scenery with a steady stream of cars and motorhomes. But the shoulder is generous and you'll soon be immersed in your own world, seeing this grand stretch of the Rockies at its proper, leisurely pace. Indeed, you may wish to extend the trip to a week or more, taking short breaks or days off the bike to sample some of the fine hikes along the way. The best way to avoid the hordes is to go in late spring or fall. If you do embark on this trip during the height of the summer tourist season, try to get an early start each morning and share the road only with deer and elk.

Other than the long haul and some steep climbs, the major challenge of the Jasper-Banff trip is the logistics. Besides getting to and fro, one must choose the style of travel. The extremely organized can bring a pursuit van, driven by alternating group members, which permits cycling with only a water bottle and camera. At the other extreme, bicycle panniers can be loaded with tents, sleeping bags, stoves, clothing, and several days of food for overnighting at one of the many campgrounds along the way. The obvious drawback of thus resembling a pack horse is being slowed by all the weight. An attractive alternative is to carry a lighter load and book reservations at the well-spaced hostels, some of which are even equipped with microwave ovens. There are only a few places between Jasper and Lake Louise to buy a limited selection of groceries, so pack accordingly.

The Icefields Parkway (Highway 93) between Jasper and Lake Louise stretches for 230 glorious kilometres along the Continental Divide beneath some of the most magnificent north faces in the Rockies. Of the dozens of glaciers visible along the way, the most prominent are those of the Columbia Icefield, the largest icefield in the Rockies. As you cycle smoothly along the asphalt, consider what it must have been like for the horse pack trains that once took two weeks to cover the same distance. Even when the Icefields Parkway opened in 1940, it was but a narrow dirt track.

From Jasper, the road is mostly level as it closely follows the Athabasca River for more than 50 kilometres. The breadth of this glacially-carved valley allows extensive southern views of prominent peaks, including the solitary uplift of Edith Cavell (3363 metres), the folded red sandstones of Kerkeslin, and the distant cluster of Brussels, Christie, and Fryatt (3361 metres). The Athabasca Valley was for many years the route of the fur traders, who followed the tributary Whirlpool River to its source at Athabasca Pass to cross the Rockies. The pass, visible from a viewpoint 25 kilometres from Jasper townsite, is visited today only by industrious backpackers.

As an alternative to the Icefields Parkway, cyclists can detour onto the parallel Highway 93A, 7.5 kilometres south of Jasper. The road is shoulderless but the traffic light as you follow a winding route through the forest. Just before regaining the main highway, be sure to stop at Athabasca Falls, where the river funnels into an explosive drop down a smooth and intricately carved canyon.

A little farther along the parkway, the road passes a mineral lick frequented by mountain goats. It's a rare opportunity to see these sure-footed animals away from the steep mountain terrain they normally haunt. Closer to the Columbia Icefield, there's a roadside spot where goats can also be sometimes seen.

At 50 kilometres from Jasper, a pull-over offers views to the south of the Athabasca Valley as it swings away from the highway and climbs to its Columbia Icefield source. Your companion is now its tributary, the Sunwapta River, which follows a parallel course along the near side of the Winston Churchill Range. A few kilometres farther, a short side-road leads to Sunwapta Falls, which has carved a deep canyon in the bedrock. A small resort nearby provides meals and some groceries.

Another faithful companion, on your left, is the Endless Chain Ridge, which follows the highway for more than 20 kilometres. The ridge's uniform, dipping slopes are composed of reddish quartzites that are highly resistant to weathering. At 75 kilometres, just past the Poboktan warden station, a slide of the same quartzite rock has descended from the ridge above, leaving a jumble of pink boulders on both sides of the road.

Not far beyond, the road enters a long flat stretch along the braided channels of the Sunwapta River. The peaks of the Columbia Icefield, glimpsed at earlier viewpoints, now rise high above the valley. Enjoy this pleasant riding while you can, as the road soon begins an arduous climb, gaining 300 metres in just 4 kilometres. The gorge to the right has cut through an ancient rock slide off Mount Kitchener. To avoid this gorge, early mountaineers detoured up Tangle Creek and over Wilcox Pass to reach the Icefield.

The Columbia Icefield is the largest conglomeration of glaciers in the Canadian Rockies, covering 325 square kilometres. Its meltwaters feed rivers that eventually empty into three oceans—Pacific, Arctic, and Atlantic. The Icefield is rimmed by eleven summits exceeding 3353 metres (11,000 feet), including Mount Columbia, at 3747 metres the second highest peak in the Canadian Rockies and the highest in Alberta. This is a popular climbing area year-round, attracting ski mountaineers, ice climbers, and summer alpinists. On a clear summer's day, several groups can usually be seen, through binoculars, ascending the photogenic north flank of Mount Athabasca.

Each year, several hundred thousand visitors take the snow coach tours up onto the Athabasca Glacier, the most accessible glacier in the Rockies. Many curious tourists also walk from a nearby parking lot up onto the lower slopes, though more than one person has died in the crevasses and millwells here. Those venturing beyond the toe should be equipped with ropes, ice axes, and crampons.

No cyclist will be able to resist stopping here to admire the scenery, visit the interpretive centre, and perhaps take one of the area's excellent hikes, some guided by naturalists. Parker's Ridge, just inside Banff National Park, is one good choice. The broad trail rises in switchbacks through thinning forest to an alpine ridge overlooking the Saskatchewan Glacier, the source of the North Saskatchewan River. The slopes of Parker's Ridge are a favoured destination of early season skiers and part of the summer range, in recent years, of a large grizzly bear. (See also the Wilcox Pass trail description, page 24.)

From Parker's Ridge, the highway drops steeply past the

Nigel Pass trailhead towards the valley bottom. A viewpoint en route offers a lofty look ahead up the narrow North Saskatchewan Valley, flanked on the left by the steep wall of Cirrus Mountain. Just beyond the big bend, the road descends again to pass the Weeping Wall. In winter, the seeping water freezes to form steep columns of ice that attract expert ice climbers.

You are now following the North Saskatchewan River, the other major Columbia Icefield watershed along the parkway. Like the north-bound Athabasca, the south-flowing North Saskatchewan is braided into many channels around the silt and gravel bars deposited by glacial meltwaters. Unlike the Athabasca, the North Saskatchewan's stay in the national parks is brief, as it soon swings left along the David Thompson Highway en route for Edmonton.

The parking lot at Saskatchewan River Crossing is a good place to view two massive peaks, Mount Wilson and Mount Murchison, which rise high above the valley. Actually, both peaks are considerably lower than Mount Forbes (3612 metres), visible on a clear day to the southwest. If you have binoculars, look for mountain goats scrambling along the cliffs of Wilson. Saskatchewan River Crossing is the last stop before Lake Louise to buy a limited selection of groceries and peruse an enormous selection of tourist souvenirs.

Just past the David Thompson Highway junction are two worthwhile stops. The first is the Howse Valley viewpoint, which affords excellent views of the valley, flanked by large peaks, leading toward distant Howse Pass. Five kilometres farther along the parkway, a short trail leads down to the deeply eroded Mistaya Canyon.

If anything, the mountain scenery becomes even more formidable as you ride beneath the huge north faces of Mount Chephren (3266 metres) and Howse Peak. Believe it or not, the Chephren face has been scaled in the depths of winter. About 10 kilometres farther, past Waterfowl Lakes, is another impressive sight, the aptly-named Snowbird

Glacier on Mount Patterson.

The road now rises up a long and gruelling 8 percent grade to Bow Summit, at 2088 metres the highest point on the trip. A short walk up a trail at the pass leads to a viewpoint overlooking the stunning turquoise waters of Peyto Lake, one of the grand scenes in the Rockies.

The descent down the other side of the pass is no less compelling as you glide through a willowy alpine meadow toward Bow Lake, framed by Crowfoot Mountain and Bow Peak. As you pass the lake, look right beyond Bow Falls to catch a glimpse of the Wapta Icefield, a favourite destination of ski mountaineers, many of whom traverse the icefield via a system of four alpine huts (see Wapta Traverse in Chapter 6).

A few kilometres farther, there's a pull-off opposite the blue ice of the Crowfoot Glacier, which despite its size has retreated considerably over the past half-century. A trail leads from the parking lot up through a lovely alpine meadow to Helen Lake and beyond to Dolomite Pass, a 9-kilometre walk one way.

Beyond Mosquito Creek, the road climbs to a viewpoint overlooking Hector Lake, a long expanse of blue water named after the energetic geologist James Hector, a member of the Palliser expedition that explored the Rockies in the late 1850s. From here, it's mostly a downhill ride to the Trans-Canada Highway junction, with glimpses above the trees of the glaciated peaks around Lake Louise.

Once the townsite is reached, cyclists will want to load up on food and perhaps ride up to visit Lake Louise, still a magnificent sight despite its fame. The home stretch between Lake Louise and Banff can be tackled in a final spurt along the congested Trans-Canada or in a more leisurely and recommended ride along the Bow Valley Parkway. This latter route traverses through a dry montane forest of lodgepole pine, with views along the way of Mount Temple and Castle Mountain. (See Bow Valley Parkway cycle trip for details of the trip beyond Castle Junction.) This quiet 50-kilometre ride ends a short distance from Banff, necessitating a last dash along the Trans-Canada into the tourist mecca.

Skier on Elk Pass trail along Fox Creek.

CHAPTER SIX

Ski Trips

Introduction

One of the finest times to be in Alberta's Rocky Mountains is on a clear winter's day after a fresh snowfall. Trails and alpine meadows hiked in summer take on a new dimension under a white coat. In winter, the woods are quieter, the trails usually less busy. If you're lucky enough to descend a slope covered in unruffled powder, there's perhaps no greater exhilaration in the mountains. One of the great things about a winter ascent into the alpine is that the descent is so much faster than on foot and much easier on the knees and feet.

All of Alberta's mountain parks offer dozens of ski trails, ranging from track-set trails to wilderness exploration. Because many ski routes follow summer hiking trails, most are usually well beaten and easily accessible from major highways.

The eastern slopes of the Rocky Mountains receive considerably less snowfall than B.C.'s interior ranges. Still, the snow pack is usually sufficient to make skiing enjoyable from late November into April, especially at higher elevations.

Weather

Temperatures can fluctuate dramatically in Alberta's Rockies, thanks to chinook winds, which blow warm air east over lee slopes. These winds can cause temperatures to rise by twenty or more degrees Celsius within hours, although their influence is more moderate in the mountains. In the aftermath of a chinook, temperatures can rise above freezing for weeks at a time.

The mercury can just as easily plunge to minus thirty or minus forty, particularly when a chinook gives way to an Arctic front. The accompanying north winds, combined with the frigid temperatures, can produce frost bite in exposed flesh within minutes.

These high winds, even on a warm day, can also hasten the onset of hypothermia, in which the body's core temperature rapidly plummets. The early symptoms of shivering can proceed quickly through lack of coordination and confusion to unconsciousness and death. As the condition advances, the only solution is externally applied heat, such as from another body.

Given the extreme variability of the weather in Alberta's Rockies, the skier's motto is "be prepared for everything."

Avalanches

Skiing above tree line in Alberta's Rockies offers unparalleled vistas but also poses considerable avalanche hazard. The light powder snow that often makes skiing so enjoyable here is also easily transported by winds and dumped onto lee slopes. As well, the relatively thin snow pack is susceptible to wide swings in temperature, which can create layers of instability. Be particularly wary after a large snowfall, especially when accompanied by high winds and sudden temperature changes.

Before embarking on back country ski trips, contact the warden's or park ranger's office nearest to your destination (see the information numbers listed in the introduction at the front of the book). Also phone the Canadian Avalanche Centre at 1-800-667-1105 for a recorded message about avalanche conditions in Alberta and British Columbia.

When travelling in avalanche terrain, stick to valley bottoms or along ridges above suspicious slopes. Stay well back from cornices. While skiing, remain alert for clues of potential avalanche danger. Watch for sluffs and snowballs on the snow surface or signs of avalanche activity on other slopes. Pay attention to "whoomphing" sounds around you and snow cracks appearing near your skis. Poking an inverted ski pole through the snow pack can expose weak layers, although digging a snow pit and conducting a shovel shear test is much more reliable.

When in avalanche terrain, always carry transceivers, shovels, and probes (or poles that convert into probes) and know how to use them. Make sure everyone in your party is carrying transceivers with compatible frequencies. Many transceivers sold now are able to transmit and receive both frequencies—2.275 kHz, the old frequency, and 457 kHz, the new frequency.

Avalanche safety is a complex subject and those interested in pursuing back country skiing should enrol in an avalanche course, available through outdoor clubs and city recreation programs. An excellent reference book is *Avalanche Safety for Skiers and Climbers*, by Tony Daffern (Rocky Mountain Books).

Those intending to do much alpine skiing should also consider courses on building snow shelters, navigating with a map and compass, wilderness first aid (especially valuable in winter for dealing with hypothermia and frostbite), and crevasse rescue.

Ratings

The routes described in this chapter are back country ski trips, usually on trails broken by oneself or other skiers. Nearly all these trips involve a significant amount of elevation gain, and hence a fair bit of downhill skiing. Many of the routes rise above tree line, exposing skiers to beautiful alpine areas but also to avalanche danger and potential route finding difficulties.

Thus this is not a beginner's guide to cross-country skiing. It is assumed that those attempting these trips know the basics of striding and gliding, of waxing, and of getting up and down hills. It also assumes they have the stamina for, in most cases, a full day's outing.

Moderate: Generally, trips of about half a day—less than 12 kilometres return, with 300 metres or less of elevation gain. The trails, if not groomed, are well travelled and fairly wide. No avalanche hazard along the trail, although some may exist in the surrounding terrain.

Intermediate: Usually a full day's outing, involving elevation gains of up to 600 metres and return distances of up to 25 kilometres. Avalanche hazard may periodically exist along the trail, although the specific route description does not involve skiing up or down avalanche slopes. Skins may be required. Skiers should be able to safely and efficiently manoeuvre downhill.

Advanced: A full day's outing and perhaps an overnight trip. Often no longer than intermediate trips but definitely exposing skiers to avalanche hazards and route finding challenges. Glacier travel may be involved. Skiers should be fit, self reliant, and experienced in travelling in a variety of alpine conditions.

Ski Mountaineering: Several days of glacier travel. Involves all the risks of advanced trips but in a remote setting. See the Wapta Traverse trip for more details.

Ski Equipment Check-list

* Skis—Lightweight fibreglass, metal-edged touring ski with enough sidecut to assist in turning. There are

also many permutations of specialized telemark skis, which are heavier and expensive but turn better.

- Boots—Heavier duty leather (usually black), above the ankle, with a mountaineering tread. Double boots are good for those with cold feet or for winter camping. High, stiff telemark boots may hobble you on longer trips.
- Bindings—A simple, heavy-duty cable binding is adjustable, provides lateral stability, doesn't tear up boots, and is practically unbreakable. Always carry at least one spare cable.
- Spare pole basket and ski tip (optional)
- Poles—Sturdy, metal pole with powder baskets. Those that convert into avalanche probes are usually good.
- Climbing skins
- Transceiver—An expensive necessity for all intermediate and advanced trips. If you're buying or renting, look for ones with dual frequencies to ensure compatibility with others on your trips.
- Avalanche shovel—Also used to dig snow shelters
- Avalanche probe poles

Clothing

Most people stay surprisingly warm while skiing. The problem is when they stop, and the sweat turns to ice. The solution lies in layering—wearing a number of clothing layers that can be removed or added as needed to stay warm and dry.

- First Layer—Long Underwear—Tops and bottoms of midweight polypropylene or similar synthetics, silk, or wool. Cotton wicks away heat, not moisture, and should be avoided.
- Second layer—Wool sweater or a pile or fleece jacket with a full zipper; it's warm and dries quickly. Pants—Knickers (wool-nylon blend sheds snow), bib pants, or Goretex pants. Some skiers wear a full body suit of quick-dry nylon.

- Third Layer—Weatherproof jacket and pants
- Back-up Layer—Down- or synthetic-fill jacket that packs small; preferably with hood.
- Mitts—Two layers, wool or pile on inside and weatherproof on outside. Carry a spare pair of inner mitts or gloves. A thin pair of gloves is handy for eating lunch or fiddling with zippers or packs.
- Toque—Wool or shelled fleece
- Balaclava or neck warmer
- Neoprene face mask—Can save face from frostbite, especially in open areas
- Water bottle—Fill with hot water and wrap in parka hood
- Sun cream—At least 15 SPF
- Glacier glasses
- Repair kit—Should contain a Phillips screw driver for tightening loose binding screws, pliers for binding repairs, a spare bale or cable, a spare pole basket, quick drying glue, and some thin wire.

MOOSE LAKE LOOPS

• **Rating:** Moderate • **Distance:** 8 kilometres return • **Time:** About 2 hours • **Elevation Gain:** 100 metres (330 feet) • **Topo Map:** 83 C/12 Athabasca Falls • **Access:** Drive 5 kilometres east of Jasper townsite on Highway 16 and take the Maligne Lake road for 45 kilometres to its terminus in the far parking lot. The trail, which initially follows the Bald Hills fire road, is nearby, beside the access road to a warden's station.

THE MOOSE LAKE loops provide a fine introduction to cross-country skiing in the mountains. The track-set route is easy, the terrain rolling, and the Maligne Lake setting spectacular. Bring your camera and a picnic lunch and enjoy the famous scenery.

Bull moose guarding the trailhead to the Moose Lake Loop.

This route loosely combines the Moose Lake and Upper Moose Lake trails. These are two of the five groomed loop trails in the Maligne Lake area. Any can be skied in a few hours; all are recommended as pleasant ski outings for the novice or intermediate cross-country skier.

As if on cue, an enormous bull moose appeared at the trailhead when I skied the Moose Lake loops. It actually got down on its front knees, like a camel, as I approached. This, it turned out, was not in deference to me but an efficient means of nibbling at the salt deposited by a Canadian Parks Service road-sanding truck. More often in this area, moose can be spotted up to their haunches in snowy meadows, nipping the buds off willows. On this loop, one snowy depression is often trampled by grazing animals.

The Moose Lake loop is best followed in a counter-clockwise direction so as to avoid collisions with other skiers on short hills. The trail begins by following the Bald Hills fire road for 250 metres. Turn left and follow the undulating track through fairly thick forest, which in midwinter blocks much of the sun. This is classic cross-country terrain through small, rolling hills, with sufficient flat stretches to allow for striding and gliding.

About 600 metres down this trail, take a short detour to the left and coast down through the trees to reach Moose Lake. The lake is nestled in heavy forest, with Leah and Samson peaks providing a spectacular white backdrop. After admiring the view, return to the junction and continue along the Upper Moose Lake loop, turning left at a junction. The right-hand trail leads to the distant Maligne Pass, a major undertaking for advanced back country skiers equipped with overnight gear.

The Upper Moose Lake trail now descends gently through a small valley dotted with large boulders, some of which have sprouted sizable trees. Soon, the forest opens to reveal the edge of snowy Maligne Lake, the largest glacier-fed lake in the Canadian Rockies. Many of the surrounding mountains were named by American Mary Schaffer, who reached the lake in 1908 and was awestruck by its beauty. Samson Peak, to the southeast, was named for the Stoney Indian, Samson Beaver, who told Schaffer how to find the lake. Directly across the lake is Leah Peak, named after Beaver's wife, where wintering mountain goats can sometimes be seen on the steep slopes.

While the lake is heavily visited by summer tourists, many bound by boat for Samson Narrows, it is equally impressive in winter, when a party of skiers can often gaze in solitude down its dazzling expanse of white. The trail follows the winding west shoreline of Maligne Lake, skirting a few enormous boulders, as it completes the loop back to the parking lot.

ELK PASS

• **Rating:** Moderate • **Distance:** 12.5 kilometres return • **Time:** 4–5 hours • **Elevation Gain:** 245 metres (800 feet) • **Topo Map:** 82 J/11 Kananaskis Lakes • **Access:** From the Trans-Canada Highway, drive 50.5 kilometres south on Highway 40, turn right and follow the Kananaskis Lakes Trail for another 12.3 kilometres to the Elk Pass parking lot.

THE ELK PASS loop is one of the best track-set ski trails in the Canadian Rockies. The snowfall is plentiful, the climb to the pass moderate, and the views splendid. In all, it's a great and safe introduction to skiing in the mountains, with a few steep hills thrown in for excitement. The only blight on this trip is a power line that briefly intrudes along the trail.

Elk Pass is among the highest and most popular of the many groomed ski trails in Peter Lougheed Provincial Park. Although rated as one of the harder trips in the park, it is forgiving by back country standards, with a wide trail along an old fire road and almost no risk of avalanches. The trail retains its snow cover from late November until well into April, making this a favourite Kananaskis Country destination throughout the ski season. Because of its relatively short length, Elk Pass is a good choice on a warm winter's day, when a picnic lunch can be laid out on the melting snow.

From the parking lot, the adequacy of one's wax selection is immediately tested on a steep hill that will likely require some herring-boning. If you're starting late, keep a watchful eye above for kamikaze skiers descending. This wide track follows a power line carrying electricity from the Kananaskis Valley into British Columbia via Elk Pass.

The trail soon crests the hill, offering views south toward Elk Pass over the steep Fox Creek Valley. All the hard-won elevation is immediately lost as you descend steeply into the forested valley, though the track is sufficiently wide and smooth to allow snowplowing. At 2 kilometres, ignore the

Hydroline Trail to the left (that's the return route) and keep following Fox Creek through the woods. Make sure you stay on the main trail, avoiding any short cuts to the left that traverse underneath a steep avalanche slope.

The route soon breaks out of the enclosed forest and commences a gentle climb alongside Fox Creek. Shortly after the trail departs the creek, two junctions are passed in quick succession. From the second, a spur trail heads right through a clearing and climbs through forest to the top of Blueberry Hill, which provides stellar views over Upper Kananaskis Lake. This detour is a fine side-trip of an hour or more for intermediate skiers who can negotiate the descent, on the return, through tighter trees.

Otherwise, continue along the Elk Pass trail as it climbs east through rolling forest to the low pass, one of three parallel passes that cross into British Columbia. Elk Pass is a good place to stop for lunch and admire the views along the Elk Range. The range acts as a long rock barrier between the pass and the parallel valley containing Highway 40 near Highwood Pass.

Just south of this clearing is the boundary to B.C.'s Elk Lakes Provincial Park. Although the two Elk Lakes are a popular summer destination, it's nearly another 5 kilometres of skiing to reach them, with the strong likelihood of having to break trail.

From Elk Pass, you can return the same way, enjoying the pleasantly fast run back down to the Fox Creek junction. To make a loop of the trip, pole your way northwest along the open Hydroline Trail. Yet another option awaits the intrepid, the switchbacking spur trail to the right up to a high lookout. Most skiers will be content to carry on down the Hydroline Trail, which makes an exciting descent through trees to rejoin the Elk Pass trail. From here, it's a short but steep climb back up a hill and then another fast ride down to the parking lot.

CHESTER LAKE

• **Rating:** Moderate • **Distance:** 9.5 kilometres return • **Time:** About 4 hours • **Elevation Gain:** 300 metres (1000 feet) • **Topo Map:** 82 J/14 Spray Lakes Reservoir • **Access:** From the Trans-Canada Highway, drive 50.5 kilometres south on Highway 40 to a junction. Turn right and drive 22.5 kilometres north on the Smith-Dorrien-Spray Trail to the Chester Lake parking lot. Alternatively, drive 45 kilometres south of Canmore on the Smith-Dorrien-Spray Trail. The trailhead is at the north end of the parking lot behind the washrooms.

THE ROUTE TO Chester Lake provides an excellent introduction to the splendours of back country skiing in the Canadian Rockies. The distance is short, the trail generally wide, and the alpine meadows superb. Reach those meadows on a calm, sunny day when the powdery snow is sparkling and you'll be hooked for good.

The uninitiated should be forewarned that the approach

Approaching Chester Lake with Gusty Peak in the background.

is steadily uphill, requiring good waxing and occasional herring-boning. In a few spots, the descent is through tighter trees, though good snow plowing technique should see you safely down to the lower, open track. Overall, the route is fairly forgiving.

Intermediate back country skiers can happily spend several hours skiing the slopes above and beyond Chester Lake. Those who do must have experience in avalanche terrain. For practiced skiers, the run down to the car can prove an exciting, continuous descent, though they should keep their speed in check to avoid collisions with those ascending. This is one of the more popular ski destinations in the Rockies, so try to get an early start to avoid the crowds, especially on weekends.

From the trailhead, follow the track-set ski trail to the left. At a junction, take the right fork; the left is the descent route. This well-beaten track takes a winding course as it climbs steadily up old logging roads. The exertion will soon have you stripping off clothing and perhaps checking the grip of your wax. Periodically, openings in the trees provide glimpses of the peaks across the valley that line the Burstall Creek drainage.

At a level junction where the descent trail is rejoined, the route abandons the wide road for a trail that climbs through spruce forest. The thick forest is twice interrupted by small clearings, one of which contains several large alpine larch trees. Soon enough, a long, open valley is gained that follows Chester Creek, lying buried beneath a blanket of snow. Sometimes, one can see winter campers in these meadows practicing the art of digging snow caves or building igloos.

At the end of this beautiful meadow is Chester Lake, tucked below the west flank of Mount Chester. Most skiers stop for lunch beside the lake, where they can admire the scenery, fend off larcenous gray jays, and watch occasional telemarkers carving turns on the slopes across the lake.

After lunch, it's worth clambering up a short trail through

trees west of the lake. There, in a clearing, sits an unusual collection of large limestone boulders which, draped in snow, will have you reaching for your camera. Experienced skiers seeking further adventure often carry on through the trees to tackle slopes in the lower Three Lakes Valley. These should only be skied when the avalanche hazard is low.

Most skiers are content to return the way they came, either snowplowing or making skid turns down through the trees. Once this narrower trail is safely navigated back to the logging road junction, continue straight ahead. The descent is almost continuous on this broad and generally smooth track, and in almost no time you are back at the parking lot.

SUNSHINE MEADOWS

• **Rating:** Moderate to Intermediate • **Distance:** About 20 kilometres return • **Time:** 6–7 hours • **Elevation Gain:** 600 metres (1970 feet) • **Topo Map:** 82 O/4 Banff • **Access:** From the west Banff townsite interchange, drive 8.3 kilometres west on the Trans-Canada Highway to the Sunshine interchange. Take the Sunshine ski area road for 9 kilometres to its terminus and park in the farthest lot, past the gondola station. The trailhead is on the left, at the bottom of the nearby ski out run. • **Note:** This trip is an easier and much shorter outing if you buy a full lift ticket for Sunshine Village, which enables you to take the gondola and then the Standish chairlift to the top of the mountain. As of this writing, Sunshine Village no longer sells a one-way lift ticket, meaning one must pay an exorbitant fee for a single ride. It also no longer track sets any ski trails in the Sunshine Meadows. For up-to-date information, phone Sunshine Village at 762-6500.

ON A CLEAR WINTER'S day, the Sunshine Meadows are one of the most glorious places to be in the Canadian Rockies. This lofty alpine perch overlooks a panorama of peaks stretching to Mount Assiniboine, the Matterhorn of the Rockies. One can ski for many kilometres on an excellent snow pack along the Continental Divide with little gain in elevation. Just make sure you pick a fine day, as the alpine meadows are subject to whiteouts that can quickly turn delight into misery.

From the parking lot trailhead, ski some 6.5 kilometres up the ski out run to Sunshine Village. This stretch gains more than 500 metres; climbing skins are optional. Allow up to two hours to reach the main lodge. If you take the lower ski out run, angle left up a short mogul hill, once past the Healy Pass turn-off, to gain a wide track. Keep an eye out for descending downhillers and resort snowmobiles.

In the trees across from the main lodge is a warden's cabin, where current avalanche conditions can be checked, especially if you plan to explore any of the steeper slopes off the meadows. Those who do should be properly equipped—and trained—for travelling in avalanche terrain. Continue up the ski hill directly behind the warden's cabin, taking the easiest angle to reach the crest of the Great Divide. This lofty spot (2300 metres) provides a good overview of the ski resort, in operation since the early 1930s.

As you head past the resort boundaries, the clamour of civilized skiing is left behind. In its place is a great expanse of rolling meadows and ridges that stretch for nearly 8 kilometres to Citadel Pass. In winter, the abundant wild flowers for which Sunshine Meadows is famous lie dormant under one of the deepest snow packs in Alberta's Rockies. But this undulating alpine terrain can be equally as stunning when the snow is glinting like diamonds under a bright sun. By contrast, the stunted and often gnarled trees that dot the meadows give evidence of how harsh life can be in this high, exposed environment.

From the divide, the route ventures briefly into B.C.'s Mount Assiniboine Provincial Park and left of Rock Isle Lake before crossing back into Banff National Park. From here, one has the option of wandering through the meadows or making short telemark runs on treed slopes.

If time permits, industrious skiers can head southeast toward Citadel Pass. The terrain is mostly level as the route passes through the odd stand of alpine larch, fir, and spruce. From a rise below Quartz Peak, the views are superb of Mount Assiniboine, at 3618 metres (11,870 feet) the highest peak in the southern Canadian Rockies. From this rise, the route drops slightly to cross Howard Douglas Lake and then carries on another 3 kilometres to the pass, left of Citadel Peak. Experienced back country skiers, equipped with overnight gear, occasionally continue over Citadel Pass en route for Magog Lake in Mount Assiniboine Provincial Park. The descent beyond the pass, however, is highly susceptible to avalanches.

As an alternative destination, ski mountaineers sometimes follow the higher ridge, from beyond Rock Isle Lake, up the two Quartz Peaks. The second and higher peak requires a bit of scrambling on foot and perhaps an ice axe. The views from this ridge encompass the peaks around Assiniboine as well as those of Kootenay National Park to the west.

Return the same way, making telemark or skid turns down the easier slopes to Sunshine Village, where a hot chocolate or beer can be quaffed before heading down the ski out. On the descent, make frequent shoulder checks to avoid being run over by speeding downhillers.

PARADISE VALLEY—GIANT STEPS

• **Rating:** Moderate to Intermediate • **Distance:** 20 kilometres return • **Time:** About 6 hours • **Elevation Gain:** 350 metres (1150 feet) • **Topo Map:** 82 N/8 Lake Louise • **Access:** From the Trans-Canada Highway, drive 2.4 kilometres through the town of Lake Louise on the road up to Lake Louise. Park in the small plowed area along the start of the Moraine Lake

Skiing across Paradise Creek with Mount Sheol in the background.

Road, which is closed in winter and serves as the initial stretch of the trip.

THE ROUTE INTO Paradise Valley is one of the most enjoyable ski outings in Banff National Park. This is a wonderful trip after a snowfall, when the trees along the trail are decked in white and sometimes doubled over under their winter weight. Novice back country skiers can turn around at any point along the way, while the more energetic can explore past the Giant Steps to the end of the valley.

The hills are fairly moderate on this route and thus climbing skins should be unnecessary. The uninitiated, however, will find the final return descent through trees quite exhilarating. All skiers continuing for any distance up Paradise Valley should carry transceivers and shovels as several avalanche run-outs are crossed.

From the parking area, ski past the barrier and follow the Moraine Lake Road, which is track set all the way to the lake. After nearly 2 kilometres, however, the Paradise Valley trail cuts right into the woods; if you reach the Paradise Valley parking lot, you've gone a couple of hundred metres too far.

From the road, the narrower trail ascends gently through a thick forest of spruce and alpine fir. At a short dip in the trail, ignore a well-beaten path to the right, which leads to Chateau Lake Louise, and proceed straight ahead. Presently the trail detours briefly to the north before turning left at a junction and climbing to the crest of a forested hill above Paradise Creek.

The trail begins a gentle descent through trees along the lower slopes of Saddle Mountain, emerging briefly out of the woods to cross a snow-packed bridge over Paradise Creek. On a clear day, this is a good place to stop for refreshments and enjoy the warmth of the sun as it briefly ascends above the high peaks flanking the valley. From this clearing, one can see the summit of Saddle Mountain to the north and the steep flank of Sheol Mountain to the west. Ahead, and to the left, the immense, glacier-capped north face of Mount Temple rises above the valley.

After briefly following the south side of the creek, the trail crosses again to the north side. Keep moving smartly as you cross the run-out zones of two major avalanche paths that descend from Sheol Mountain. Soon, a short summer trail leads left to Lake Annette. If you don't mind thrashing up a fairly steep hill through tighter trees, you can gain an overview of the lake and a closer look at Temple.

Those interested in further adventures can seek out the Giant Steps, where a tributary of Paradise Creek flows over several flat quartzite steps. In winter, the ice and snow here assume interesting shapes. Beyond the Lake Annette junction, it is often easier to ski along or near the creek for a couple of kilometres. The Giant Steps are not always easily found in winter as the broken trail often ends well before they are reached. One can either forge up the right-hand fork where the stream splits or contour around from the left.

If time and energy permit, a further path can be blazed to the head of the valley, below the impressive Horseshoe Glacier. In summer, a trail leads left up scree slopes to the lofty Sentinel Pass, providing access to the Valley of the Ten Peaks. This avalanche-prone route is definitely not recommended in winter. Across the valley to the west stands The Mitre, from where several mountaineers looked down into this green valley in 1894 and declared it paradise.

BALD HILLS

• **Rating:** Moderate to Intermediate • **Distance:** 11 kilometres return • **Time:** 3–5 hours • **Elevation Gain:** 480 metres (1575 feet) • **Topo Map:** 83 C/12 Athabasca Falls • **Access:** Drive 5 kilometres east of Jasper townsite on Highway 16 and take the Maligne Lake road for 45 kilometres to its terminus in

Maligne Lake and surrounding peaks from the Bald Hills.

the far parking lot. The signed trailhead is nearby, beside
the access road to a warden's station.

ON A CLEAR, CALM day, the Bald Hills may well be the
finest ski destination in the Jasper area. The lookout provides a commanding view over Maligne Lake and a sweep
of mountain ranges dusted in white. Skiers can also happily spend several hours exploring the rolling subalpine
meadows or testing their telemark skills on moderate slopes.

One needn't be an experienced back country skier to enjoy
this alpine splendour. The trail, while steadily uphill, is relatively short and follows a wide road to the lookout. There
are few places in the Rockies that offer so much for so little
effort. But those who depart the beaten track for steeper
slopes are venturing onto avalanche terrain and should be
properly trained and equipped for such hazards.

The trail follows an old fire road throughout. In winter,
this fairly mundane approach is transformed by deep snow
that covers the road and cloaks the flanking lodgepole pines.
On a sunny day, the dappled light through this open forest
is indeed magical.

From the parking lot, the trail rises gently, passing a corral and related Canadian Parks Service buildings. The initial
stretch, providing access to several of the Maligne Lake ski
loops, is track set, allowing for orderly two-way traffic. At
about 3 kilometres, a trail to the right is passed. It leads to
Evelyn Creek and, beyond, the Skyline Trail, one of the best
backpacks in the Canadian Rockies. Although the Skyline
is seldom tackled in winter, the bowls beyond the nearby
Little Shovel Pass provide exceptional alpine skiing for
advanced back country skiers.

The fire road route now climbs in earnest through an
increasingly subalpine forest of spruce and fir. Good waxing and perhaps a bit of herring-boning should see you up
the steeper sections. Ignore a steep short cut to the left and
stay on the main trail, which winds around the back side
of the hills. The reward for this effort is a view above the
trees to the alpine terrain surrounding Little Shovel Pass.
To the south, the jagged peaks of the Colin Range appear,
as do the mountains of the Elizabeth Range, closer at hand
to the east.

These views are but an appetizer for what lies ahead. After
swinging around the west side of the Bald Hills, the route
climbs to tree line and the abandoned lookout. Suddenly,
one is confronted by a stunning vista down frozen Maligne
Lake to its 14-kilometre point at Samson Narrows. Flanking the lake are Leah and Samson peaks, on the left, and
the twin peaks of Mount Unwin and Mount Charlton, on
the right. Beyond the lake lies Mount Brazeau, at 3470 metres
the highest peak in the Jasper area.

In winter, the only vestige of the old fire lookout is a hitching post for horses. Skiers can tie their boards to the rail
and, if the weather's good, enjoy a leisurely lunch. I spent
nearly an hour here at minus twenty-five degrees Celsius
on a cloudless day when there was not a breath of wind.

The surrounding meadows are enticing and well worth
touring for another hour or so. One can also ski onto the

higher of these naked hills, though caution should be exercised in this avalanche terrain. Telemark opportunities abound on gentle slopes that descend through well-spaced trees.

There are several options for the return. Telemarkers can carve their own route through the trees to regain the fire road, though they should avoid steeper slopes farther down the east side of the hills. Most skiers will choose to return the way they came.

The descent is fast and nearly continuous; a two-hour ascent is retraced in less than half an hour. The road is sufficiently wide, and usually well beaten, to allow for snow-plowing, tight telemarking, or, if you dare, schussing. In all cases, skiers should control their speed so as to avoid collisions with ascending skiers, who may be scattered across the trail with their heads down. At several places on the descent, there are impressive views of the wedge-shaped Samson Peak, framed by lodgepole pines.

SKOKI LODGE

• **Rating:** Intermediate • **Distance:** 25 kilometres return • **Time:** About 7 hours • **Elevation Gain:** 475 metres (1560 feet) • **Topo Maps:** 82 N/8 Lake Louise and 82 N/9 Hector Lake • **Access:** From the Lake Louise interchange on the Trans-Canada Highway, drive 2 kilometres up the Lake Louise Ski Area access road. Turn right onto a gravel road, which is followed for 1.1 kilometres to the Fish Creek parking lot. • **Note:** Skiers can usually catch a 10 a.m. shuttle bus (currently $5) from the parking lot to Temple Lodge. Phone Lake Louise Ski Area at 522-3555 for up-to-date information. This trip assumes a start from Temple Lodge. Those wishing to save money or get an earlier start, can ski up the ski out from the parking lot, adding 4 kilometres, 300 vertical metres, and a little more than an hour to the trip.

Skoki Lodge.

A HISTORIC SKI route reputedly visited by ghosts, the trip into Skoki Lodge provides a good introduction to back country touring for the intermediate skier. The route is mostly above tree line, crosses two gentle passes, and poses little avalanche hazard. After a fresh snowfall, it also offers some pleasant downhill skiing.

Strong skiers can make the return trip in a long day. Many take a more leisurely approach and spend a night or two at the historic Skoki Lodge, where comfortable lodgings and all meals are provided. The shuttle bus trip to Temple Lodge is included in the nightly fee. For information, call Lake Louise Ski Area at 522-3555.

To reach the trailhead, traverse across the lower ski runs above Temple Lodge, an outlying day-use facility of the ski resort. Just before the lodge, there is a warden's office, where current avalanche conditions can be checked.

The ski resort is quickly left behind as one follows a well-beaten trail through a forest of spruce and alpine fir. After about 2 kilometres of gently rising through woods, the trail opens onto meadows that provide views of glaciated Slate

Range mountains such as Ptarmigan Peak, Pika Peak, and Richardson Peak.

Just beyond, on the left bank of Corral Creek, is Halfway Hut, so named because it marked the halfway point for early skiers heading from the Lake Louise train station to Skoki Lodge. Today, it serves as a dark and chilly rest spot for hikers and skiers. Ghosts of skiers lost in avalanches are said to haunt this valley at night.

If time permits, eager telemarkers might choose to break trail northwest from the hut towards Hidden Lake. Part way up this trail, a short, treed slope on the left always seems to have fluffy powder, even when adjacent hills are crusted by wind. While higher slopes are also tempting, they are more prone to avalanches.

From Halfway Hut, the trail rises moderately through trees and boulders to the aptly named Boulder Pass. This low rise overlooks Ptarmigan Lake ahead and provides distant views southwest to Mount Temple and Mount Victoria. The pass is frequented by pikas and ptarmigans, but in winter the most constant companion is a gusty wind. Indeed, as one crosses Ptarmigan Lake and the open valley beyond, winds lashing the snow can easily produce whiteout conditions, which accounts for the route posts planted along the way.

Once across Ptarmigan Lake, the route begins to traverse left up to Deception Pass. It's the saddle on the right, below the west shoulder of Fossil Mountain, not the one on the left below Ptarmigan Peak. This is the only real climb of the approach. While climbing skins will help under certain snow conditions, one can always do without by switchbacking up the hill.

The pass overlooks the Skoki Valley and Skoki Mountain to the north. Skoki is allegedly a Stoney Indian word for swamps; there are several in the vicinity of the lodge. The dolomite rocks of Skoki and Fossil mountains are both from the Skoki Formation, in which fossilized snails are commonly found.

From the pass, contour slightly to the right before descending moderate slopes to Skoki Valley. The descent is fast and sustained, with lots of space between widely scattered trees in which to turn. If you are blessed with powder, it can be a heavenly run down. If the snow is crusty, pick your way down as best as possible. The packed trail is regained near the bottom of the hill. Follow it or the creek to Skoki Lodge, ignoring a fork to the right that ventures off between Skoki and Fossil mountains.

Skoki Lodge was built in 1930 by Clifford White and Cyril Paris as one of the first back country ski lodges in the Canadian Rockies. Back then, it was a popular destination for skiers, who schussed down the hills with their long skis and poles. Samples of this early gear, as well as a number of excellent black-and-white photos on the walls, help recapture the spirit of the times. So does the building itself, with its log construction, large fireplace, and lack of electricity. It is a popular overnight destination for intermediate skiers, eager to escape the conveniences and frantic pace of modern society.

For a small fee, the friendly staff will serve tea and cakes to day-visitors. After several hours of exertion, such refreshments never tasted so good. If this is a day-trip, don't relax for too long. It's still a fair distance back to the car, and the return trip should be commenced by early afternoon to avoid a final descent in darkness.

The biggest challenge is climbing up the long hill to Deception Pass that was so pleasantly descended an hour or so ago. As you climb, imagine the fortitude of the skiers who used to pack huge loads of provisions into Skoki all the way from Lake Louise. In the lodge, there are "then and now" photos of one such packer and mountain guide, 80-something Ken Jones, who at last report was still skiing into Skoki and Assiniboine on his long wooden skis. Once the pass is crested, the rest of the return is nearly all gently downhill, save the initial plunge down the ski out. Make sure you stop at the Fish Creek parking lot, where the ski out crosses a road.

HEALY PASS

• **Rating:** Intermediate • **Distance:** 18.5 kilometres return • **Time:** About 6–7 hours • **Elevation Gain:** 625 metres (2050 feet) • **Topo Map:** 82 O/4 Banff • **Access:** From the west Banff townsite interchange, drive 8.3 kilometres west on the Trans-Canada Highway to the Sunshine interchange. Take the Sunshine ski area road for 9 kilometres to its terminus and park in the farthest lot, past the gondola station. The trailhead is on the left, at the bottom of the nearby ski out run.

THE EXPANSIVE MEADOWS below Healy Pass provide an excellent destination for intermediate back country skiers. The snow flies early and often here along the Continental Divide, next door to the Sunshine ski resort. This is thus a popular pre-Christmas outing for those wishing to tune up their legs and practice rusty telemarking skills. Best of

Skier at Healy Pass overlooking Pharaoh Peaks.

all, skiers can spend hours exploring the many bowls and ridges in this alpine wonderland.

It's best to save this trip for a clear, calm day as blowing snowstorms can easily produce whiteout conditions above tree line and force a hasty retreat. If you're tackling this trip during the short days of December, try to get an early start, which will allow for more time in the meadows. Although good waxing may get you up the steeper sections near the end of the wooded trail, climbing skins are a definite asset. Be sure to turn your avalanche transceiver on at the parking lot, as people have been buried and lost their lives on the approach trail.

From the parking lot, ski up the packed trail of the Sunshine ski out run, keeping an eye out for descending downhill skiers. As you ascend, look right to the south walls of Mount Bourgeau, which in most winters is smeared by two frozen waterfalls that attract ice climbers. Within a kilometre, take a subsidiary trail to the right that descends to a bridged crossing of Healy Creek. The trail now climbs pleasantly through a forest thick with alpine fir and Engelmann spruce.

At 3 kilometres, the creek is crossed again, and the trail begins traversing through forest interrupted by several avalanche clearings. Although these low-angled clearings are generally safe, they are no place to dally. Occasionally, massive avalanches break off from high above and sweep down to the creek.

A small campground is reached at 5.5 kilometres. Advanced skiers sometimes break trail up a drainage to the right, which leads to Bourgeau Meadows. A summer trail, seldom used in winter, heads left to Simpson Pass and the Sunshine ski hill. Your destination lies straight ahead on a trail that now begins a more serious climb to subalpine meadows.

Just beyond a stand of larch trees, the rolling meadows below Healy Pass are reached. The slopes here are sufficiently gentle for novice telemarkers to safely practice their turns. By bearing slightly to the right, Healy Pass is soon reached.

At 2300 metres, the pass provides excellent views along the Continental Divide, which separates Alberta from British Columbia. The long ridge extending to the south is the Monarch Rampart, leading to The Monarch. On a clear day, one can see all the way southeast to the pyramid-shaped summit of Mount Assiniboine, one of the alpine landmarks of the Rockies.

To the northwest, Egypt Lake is visible at the foot of the Pharaoh Peaks. Obviously, someone with the Topographical Survey, which named these parts in the early 1900s, had an affinity for things Egyptian; the other nearby lakes are called Scarab, Mummy, Sphinx, and Eohippus. To the northeast is Mount Bourgeau, perhaps more appropriately named for the French botanist who collected more than 1200 plant species during his travels with the Palliser expedition in the late 1850s. Incidentally, the pass you are standing on is named after John Healy, a one-time Montana sheriff and mining prospector in the Rockies.

For experienced back country skiers, the options from Healy Pass are numerous. One can swing northeast and explore the meadows below Bourgeau, taking care on steeper avalanche slopes. Alternatively, the wind-blasted ridge of the Monarch Ramparts can be followed south to where skiers can descend on gentler slopes to Eohippus Lake and break trail back to the main trail.

Many skiers descend the northwest slopes to Egypt Lake. Some stay overnight in an alpine cabin, while others carry on to pick up the Redearth Creek trail back to the Trans-Canada Highway, a 29-kilometre trip in total that requires a second vehicle or hitching a ride back to the Sunshine parking lot.

Most skiers return the way they came. The initial descent through the trees is fairly steep and exciting, perhaps too much so for those who must snowplow on paining thighs.

Keep your speed in check, especially if conditions are icy, to avoid nasty spills or collisions with trees or ascending skiers. The lower run down through forest is also sustained but at a more moderate pace.

MACCARIB PASS

• **Rating:** Intermediate to Advanced • **Distance:** 25 kilometres return • **Time:** 7–9 hours • **Elevation Gain:** 700 metres (2300 feet) • **Topo Maps:** 83 D/16 Jasper and 83 D/9 Amethyst Lakes • **Access:** Drive 7.5 kilometres south of Jasper on Highway 93 and take Highway 93A for 2.5 kilometres. Turn right on the Marmot Basin Road, which is followed for 6.6 kilometres to a crossing of Portal Creek. Park in the small lot on the left, just before the bridge. The trailhead is reached by crossing the bridge and turning left.

THE VIEW FROM the Maccarib Pass area is one of the finest in the Canadian Rockies. Stretching across the horizon are the Ramparts—a 1000-metre-high wall of quartzite peaks rising above Amethyst Lakes. Resplendent in white, the Ramparts and the foreground of rolling meadows are a magical sight on a clear day.

The Tonquin Valley, which contains Amethyst Lakes, is one of the most popular overnight destinations in the Rockies in summer. In winter, however, the hordes of backpackers and horse pack trains have disappeared, as have the mosquitoes and mucky trails. Indeed, a midwinter's party of skiers might find themselves alone in this silent wilderness.

The trail is intermediate, at most, for much of the approach. But the ascent of Maccarib Pass, especially in whiteout conditions, can require route-finding skills. Although the grade below the pass is relatively moderate, the neighbouring slopes can pose an avalanche hazard. Those who venture to and beyond the pass should be fit and accomplished back country skiers.

Save this long trip for a clear day and start at first light, so you can savour the alpine meadows and still get back well before sundown. Pack warm clothing. The treeless pass is exposed to the elements, and in midwinter, sunlight disappears from Portal Creek by early afternoon.

Just beyond the parking lot, the trail passes an outfitter's cabin and begins to rise gently but steadily through forest. On the left, Portal Creek is a constant companion as it bubbles beneath a blanket of snow. If the snow pack is sufficiently deep, it may be possible to ski all the way up the creek.

Within a few kilometres, the impressive Peveril Peak, named after Walter Scott's novel, *Peveril of the Peak*, rises into view. The ensuing forest of mature, well-spaced pine and spruce allows nearly continuous views up and down the valley. Behind, across the broad Athabasca Valley, lie the low peaks of the Maligne Range, including Mount Tekarra, a landmark near the end of the Skyline Trail. Ahead, at the end of the valley, the trees give way to the alpine heights of Maccarib Pass.

At about 4 kilometres, Portal Creek is joined by the tributary Circus Creek. Here, just before a bridged crossing of the latter, the trail should descend to follow Portal Creek. Beware of any broken trail that stays high on the right side of the valley. This latter route follows the summer trail, which traverses dangerous avalanche slopes below Peveril Peak. They should definitely be avoided.

The correct route winds for another 4 kilometres along Portal Creek's stream bed to reach a campground below the pass. This section, running between Peveril and Lectern peaks, is called The Portal for its resemblance to an entrance way.

The snow along the creek is often trampled by the meandering tracks of woodland caribou, known informally as mountain caribou at these elevations. Observant skiers may spy one of these shy animals browsing on protruding willow buds. Not surprisingly, Maccarib is a native word for caribou. I once spent a night near Maccarib Pass with biologist Kent Brown, who was scanning the meadows above the Tonquin Valley as part of a caribou research project in the Jasper area.

From the campground, the creek is followed for another couple of kilometres to tree line, near the end of the valley. The route then turns right and ascends moderate slopes toward Maccarib Pass (Grid Reference 197415). Avoid turning right up an earlier pass.

The views from Maccarib Pass encompass rolling meadows and the entrance to the Tonquin Valley, to the west. To gain the first glimpse of the Ramparts, however, it is necessary to ski a little farther west. Soon enough, Barbican Peak, Mount Geikie, and the other awesome summits along the west end of the Ramparts rise into sight.

It's hard to turn around, as the view keeps improving the farther one skis down Maccarib Creek. But keep a close eye on your watch and the weather, allowing ample time for the long return to the parking lot.

Overnight Options

This day-trip is but an appetizer to the joys of the Tonquin Valley, one of the finest overnight ski destinations in the Canadian Rockies. Those who venture into this winter wilderness can either winter camp or make bookings at one of two winter cabins.

One is a private, full-service operation, known as Dixon Lodge, at the north end of Amethyst Lakes, 23 kilometres from the Portal Creek parking lot. Phone 852-3909 in Jasper. The other is the Wates-Gibson Hut, a fine Alpine Club of Canada facility. Phone 678-3200 in Canmore. Users should be aware that the hut, located near Outpost Lake (grid reference 152353), south of Amethyst Lakes, can be hard to find.

A good three- or four-day circuit is to ski into the Tonquin via the Astoria River and exit over Maccarib Pass. The trip begins with an 11-kilometre ski up the Edith Cavell road to the Mount Edith Cavell Hostel. Phone 439-3139 in Edmonton for reservations. The next day is a 14-kilometre ski along the Astoria River to reach Wates-Gibson Hut.

It's worth spending a day or two exploring the Tonquin area—including a jaunt onto the Fraser Glacier or a tour beneath the Ramparts. Because the Ramparts follow the Continental Divide—marking the boundary between Alberta and British Columbia—the snow pack is usually excellent. From the hut, it's a 28-kilometre ski out via Maccarib Pass to the Portal Creek parking lot. Fortunately, much of that stretch is downhill.

DOLOMITE PEAK CIRCUIT

• **Rating:** Advanced • **Distance:** 19 kilometres • **Time:** 6–7 hours • **Elevation Gain:** 655 metres (2150 feet) • **Topo Map:** 82 N/9 Hector Lake • **Access:** From the Trans-Canada Highway just west of Lake Louise townsite, drive 29 kilometres north on the Icefields Parkway to a small, unmarked park-

Telemarking near Dolomite Pass.

ing lot on the right, just west of Helen Creek. The trailhead is just beyond the trees. Leave a second vehicle 5 kilometres south at Mosquito Creek, or hitchhike back to your car.

FOR EXPERIENCED BACK country skiers, this is a superb trip into the extensive alpine meadows around Dolomite Pass. Much of the route, which circumnavigates Dolomite Peak, is above tree line. On a sunny winter day, when the views extend to the Wapta Icefield and the open slopes are covered in fresh snow, there's hardly a better place to be. On the other hand, this alpine outing is hardly worth attempting if the weather is poor and should definitely be avoided if avalanche conditions are at all hazardous.

Depending on the conditions and the fitness of the party (the elevation gain exceeds 650 metres), this trip can easily take all day, so be sure to get an early start. For that reason, many skiers save this trip for the longer hours of late winter and early spring. Befitting an area above tree line and susceptible to whiteouts, this outing requires good route finding and avalanche awareness skills.

From the trailhead, switchback steeply up through trees, following a fairly obvious line if no trail has been broken. The trail then swings left along a ridge high above Helen Creek before dropping out of the trees to cross the creek. The route continues along the north side of the creek through trees interspersed with avalanche run-out slopes from Dolomite Peak high above. The creek is recrossed on a bridge below a large rock.

To avoid skiing up a narrow and steep-sided valley, angle right up through well-spaced trees. Once above tree line, follow a ridge to the right of a small drainage and contour to the right around a hill. The aim is to go up a short ramp through a break in a small cliff band to reach the crest of a low ridge. This lofty spot offers superb views south across the Bow Valley to Bow Peak and beyond, at the far end of the Waputik Icefield, to Mount Daly.

From this ridge, the route descends gently down an open slope toward Katherine Lake, allowing telemarkers to practice some low-angled turns. If the snow conditions are good, many skiers will make a couple of runs on the steeper slopes to the left. A favourite mountaineering outing is to continue left up the ridge to reach the summit of Cirque Peak, which offers extensive views of the Wapta Icefield to the southwest and the Dolomite Creek drainage to the north.

From the north end of Katherine Lake, ski past a couple of large boulders that mark the entrance to Dolomite Pass. On a clear day, this is a magical place, as one is encircled by a white blanket of rolling terrain that rises to ridges and peaks. Rather than continue on through the pass, angle right down gentle slopes into the bottom of a basin to the east.

The route now begins a steady climb to a small col between Dolomite Peak and an unnamed mountain to the northeast (grid reference 442264). The col is usually hard-packed and windswept, though I have broken trail through knee-deep powder here. If you're in luck, the steep slope on the other side of the col will be free of the breakable crust that usually guarantees a few face plants. Descend this steep upper bowl one at a time if the conditions are at all unstable.

The valley remains narrow for a kilometre or two, requiring tight turns in a few places. The grade eventually eases off, allowing for a fast descent through increasingly open meadows. In no time, you'll be back at tree line and facing a descent that is steep and a bit tricky. Choose your poison of a bumpy sidehill above a small creek (best avoided if avalanche conditions are above moderate) or a slalom run through tight trees.

Finally, the slope eases, the trees open up, and Mosquito Creek is reached. After perhaps many hours of breaking trail, it is a relief to follow a well-beaten path for the final few kilometres along the creek and down through the trees to the trail's end near the Mosquito Creek Hostel.

ROBERTSON-FRENCH LOOP

• **Rating:** Advanced • **Distance:** 20 kilometres return • **Time:** 7–8 hours • **Elevation Gain:** 990 metres (3250 feet) • **Topo Maps:** 82 J/14 Spray Lakes Reservoir and 82 J/11 Kananaskis Lakes • **Access:** From the Trans-Canada Highway, drive 50.5 kilometres south on Highway 40. Turn right and head 22.5 kilometres north on the Smith-Dorrien-Spray Trail to the trailhead at the Mud Lake parking lot. • **Note:** This loop can be followed in either direction. The counter-clockwise, Robertson-French, route is described here because it minimizes the time spent on the steep slope beneath the Robertson-Sir Douglas Col.

ON A CLEAR WINTER'S day, the lofty view over the Haig Glacier is almost certain to expand one's soul. Stretching for kilometres below a high col is an untracked sea of dazzling snow ringed by ragged peaks. It may be the closest thing to recapturing the feeling of early explorers who, upon cresting a mountain or high pass, suddenly looked down on vast

Skiers at the head of the French Glacier. Photo by Dennis Stefani.

areas of untouched wilderness.

Within a relatively short distance, this trip covers three glaciers and two provinces and rises to one of the higher, accessible cols in the Rockies. If you're in luck, you might also find enough unruffled snow to enjoy some good turns on the descent.

This is definitely a trip for ski mountaineers experienced in travelling on glaciers and in avalanche terrain. Indeed, the convex slope descending from the Robertson-Sir Douglas Col is highly susceptible to avalanches and should not be tackled if conditions are at all unsafe. While most skiers travel this route unroped, park rangers recommend appropriate gear for glacier travel be carried and used.

An early start is also suggested, as the route climbs nearly 1000 metres over the first 10 kilometres, making this a fairly long day even for fit skiers. If the weather conditions are bad as one ascends the Robertson Glacier, it's best to abandon the loop. Up here, whiteouts can be dangerous as well as miserable.

From the parking lot, cross the often windswept clearing past Mud Lake. Once in the trees, ignore the French Glacier trail to the left (that's the descent route) and follow the rolling logging road above Burstall Creek and Lakes. At road's end, follow a trail down through trees to open flats that in summer are a mass of braided streams.

Instead of proceeding straight to the equally delightful Burstall Pass, head left towards Robertson Glacier. From the flats, the glacier is clearly visible as it rises impressively to a narrow col between Mount Robertson, on the left, and Mount Sir Douglas, which at 3406 metres is the tenth highest peak in the southern Canadian Rockies. Pick the most open line through the trees, which soon give way to a narrow valley. Although the glacier appears close, there is still a considerable stretch of mounded glacial rubble to be bypassed first.

The entrance to the glacier is prone to avalanches from

both sides of the valley, although that danger eases some-what as one ascends up the glacier. At the glacier's toe, it's worth fixing climbing skins to your skis and taking fairly steep switchbacks up the snow slopes. The glacier rises in several such steps, which provide excellent telemarking on those infrequent days when the area's strong winds haven't created a crust.

Generally, stick to the right side of the valley and then, near the top, contour left towards the col. Clamber up the last slope to this rocky spot and descend a few metres on the other side to gain shelter from often fierce winds.

At a lofty 2900 metres, the col looks down on the expanse of the Haig Glacier and a ring of peaks, including Monro, LeRoy, Maude, and Jellicoe, all commemorating military figures active around World War I. Both Mount Sir Douglas, to the immediate right, and the glacier below are named after Sir Douglas Haig, who headed the British Expeditionary Force in France after that war. The Haig Glacier's meltwaters feed both the Upper Kananaskis River, which in turn feeds the Bow River, and the Palliser River, which eventually reaches the Pacific Ocean via the Kootenay and Columbia rivers.

Take great care descending the steep avalanche slope from the col to the Haig Glacier. Sometimes it's best to take your skis off and walk down beside rocks on the left. The lower, gentler slopes are often sheltered from the wind and thus much more pleasant to ski. You are now briefly in British Columbia, although Alberta is re-entered as soon as you round the corner of Mount Robertson and begin heading north down the French Glacier. The snow at the base of Robertson has been scoured into a deep, semicircular moat, a unique sight in the Rockies.

The descent down the French Glacier is fast and reasona-bly gentle, although I always seem to encounter wind-blasted slopes sculpted into small waves. There can be some route-finding problems coming off the glacier. Most skiers stay right, above French Creek, and descend through tree-covered slopes. Beyond, there are a few tight gullies to test your reflexes and low willows to threaten your ankles. Steer clear of any avalanche slopes as you descend. With luck, a party ascending the French Glacier will have left a broken trail to follow. If not, generally follow the east side of the creek until a packed trail is gained, guiding you through the final few kilometres of trees to the junction with your approach trail, just before the parking lot.

WAPTA TRAVERSE

• **Rating:** Advanced—Ski mountaineering • **Distance:** About 50 kilometres • **Time:** 3–5 days • **Elevation Gain:** 1020 metres (3350 feet) • **Topo Maps:** 82 N/9 Hector Lake, 82 N/10 Blaeberry River, and 82 N/8 Lake Louise. A weatherproof topo map showing various routes across the Wapta and Waputik icefields is published by Murray Toft and available at many outdoor shops. • **Access:** From the Trans-Canada Highway just west of Lake Louise townsite, drive 36 kilometres north

Skiing above Peter and Catherine Whyte Hut with Mount Baker on the left and Trapper Peak on the right.

on the Icefields Parkway to Bow Lake. From the parking lot, beside the highway, ski down past the red-roofed Num-ti-jah Lodge and onto Bow Lake. • **Note:** If you plan to stay in any or all of the four alpine huts along the traverse, make reservations well ahead of time through the Alpine Club of Canada. Phone 678-3200 in Canmore.

FOR EXPERIENCED SKI mountaineers, the Wapta Traverse is one of the great glacier traverses in the world. Up on this expanse of snow, the mountain vistas are superb, the opportunities for ski mountaineering and telemarking numerous, and the travelling conditions relatively safe. The traverse is made all the more enjoyable by a series of alpine cabins that allow loads to be lightened and the trip broken into a number of short days. It's the closest thing we have to the civilized traverses of Europe's Alps, but in a wilderness setting.

Popularly known as the Wapta Traverse, the trip actually embraces two icefields—the Wapta and Waputik, Stoney Indian words for, respectively, running water and mountain goat. For most of its length, the route is a high wire act along the Continental Divide, which serves as the boundary between Alberta and British Columbia. Along the way, it crosses one pass and three high cols, including the 2970-metre Balfour High Col. Needless to say, the vistas across snow and peaks are frequent and spectacular.

But before you book any huts, be forewarned that weather conditions can make this either the ski trip of a lifetime or a traverse of unmitigated misery. Many parties have spent a week in a whiteout, battered by winds and unable to make out anything beyond their ski tips. But if the weather clears, the snowy peaks thrusting out of the glacier are truly stupendous. I vividly recall a Japanese woman, after three days of storms, shriek with shocked delight upon awakening to see the dawn illuminating Mount Rhondda. The trip is best attempted from February to April, when the days are longer and warmer and the snow pack at its peak.

Anyone tackling the Wapta Traverse should be an experienced ski mountaineer, fully equipped for glacier travelling, route finding, skiing in avalanche terrain, and possibly bivouacking in bad weather. For safety reasons, a minimum party size of three is recommended. While open crevasses are not numerous for an icefield of this size, they do exist. Thus skiers should carry ropes, harnesses, and prusiks—and know how to use them. Obviously, avalanche transceivers, shovels, topo maps, compasses, and sufficient warm and weatherproof clothing should also be packed. Ice axes and crampons are suggested if ski mountaineering is planned. Some parties may choose to winter camp—either in tents or snow caves—en route rather than use the huts.

The skiing is relatively straightforward by back country standards. But the addition of a heavy pack can prove taxing on both the long climbs and the descents. Thus, skiers should have the stamina to cover the distance and the technique to handle a variety of snow conditions.

There is some argument about what constitutes the true Wapta Traverse. Some parties start from Peyto Lake, others from Bow Lake. This description begins from the latter, as the approach toward the Peyto Glacier is sometimes bereft of snow, necessitating some walking and some scrambling over a slippery rock step. As a result of the Bow Lake start, the route is somewhat circuitous, though none the less splendid. All trips end at Wapta Lake. While the traverse has been completed in a dawn-to-dusk spurt with day packs, most parties spend three to five days savouring the alpine experience or sitting out any bad weather.

From the parking lot, the route heads straight across the west end of frozen Bow Lake, which provides excellent views down the broad Bow Valley. Beyond the lake, follow a braided stream channel around a corner, cut left up through trees and traverse right below an avalanche slope. The trail drops over a small shoulder and bypasses frozen Bow Falls, a popular ice climbing destination, as it proceeds up a narrow gulley, alongside a small stream. At the end of this gulley, climb up a small bench to reach a treed slope, which is traversed until the valley opens up (climbing skins may be needed here). Aim for the glacier hanging menacingly over the end of the valley. Just before it is reached, turn right up a bowl-shaped snow ramp. Needless to say, this is no place to stop. Angle right across this ramp to reach a shoulder.

Just beyond is Bow Hut, a Hilton of public alpine lodges with a balcony, picture windows, a wood stove, separate sleeping quarters, and a large, fully equipped kitchen. It's a far cry from the old hut, a chilly tin cigar located farther up the glacier. It can take anywhere from 2.5 to 5 hours to reach the hut, depending on your load, fitness level, and the snow conditions.

Some strong parties carry on the same day to the Peter and Catherine Whyte (nee Peyto) Hut, another two or three hours beyond Bow Hut. Regardless of when you tackle that stretch, set aside at least an hour en route to ski the bowl to the right of St. Nicholas Peak. If snow conditions are good, this is one of the longest and best ski slopes in the Canadian Rockies, with enough variation in slope angle to please both novice and advanced telemarkers.

To reach the Whyte Hut, aim for the lower rim of this bowl, to the right of centre. As you crest the rim, the horizon expands dramatically to encompass the great expanse of the Wapta Icefield and the mountains that rise along its icy edges. To maintain elevation and avoid a large depression, angle left towards the shoulder of Mount Rhondda.

The high point of this climb roughly marks a significant watershed. To the north, the Peyto Glacier empties into the Mistaya River and then the North Saskatchewan River. To the east, the Bow Glacier feeds the Bow River and then the South Saskatchewan, which finally rejoins its northern namesake in the middle of the Saskatchewan prairie. Meanwhile, on the other side of Mount Rhondda, the Ayesha Glacier is depositing its meltwaters into the Blaeberry River, which feeds the Kicking Horse River and then the mighty Columbia River.

From near the Rhondda shoulder, contour back right, descending a long, gentle slope to the Whyte Hut, perched on a rock outcrop above the right side of the Peyto Glacier. The hut faces a high, snowy bowl ringed by Peyto and Trapper peaks and Mounts Baker and Rhondda, a stunning sight at dawn. After a leisurely breakfast in this spartan but cozy cabin, head back up the slope, aiming generally for the flank of St. Nicholas.

This high traverse provides not only marvellous views but also access to exceptional ski mountaineering. Many of the surrounding peaks were first climbed on foot at the turn of the century by such luminaries as Edward Whymper (who made the first ascent of the Matterhorn), John Norman Collie, James Outram, Charles Fay, and their Swiss guides.

Before St. Nicholas is reached, angle right to gain a low, windswept col between Nicholas and Mount Olive. Once over the col, contour slightly right and descend down the long gentle slope of the Vulture Glacier, taking care to not stray too far right onto an icefall. As the corner is rounded, you are confronted by one of the stellar sights in the Rockies, the north glacier rising to Mount Balfour. To the distant east is another splendid sight, the long, gentle glacier rising to Mount Hector, which at 3394 metres is the highest peak in the area. The scene is completed by the impressively folded east and south rock faces that rise to the twin summits of Mount Olive.

At the foot of the Vulture Glacier sits the new, relocated Balfour Hut, its large windows facing south toward Mount Balfour. From the hut, drop slightly to reach Balfour Pass, which marks the division between the Wapta and Waputik icefields. Cross moraines and then begin the longest climb of the trip, a vertical ascent of more than 500 metres. Follow the obvious ramp along Balfour's east slopes, travelling as quickly as possible beneath the icefalls and corniced ridges, which can send avalanches across the route at any time. Looking back, the western end of Hector Lake is visible far below.

At 2970 metres, the Balfour High Col is loftier than many mountain summits and thus offers superb views, especially south across the Waputik Icefield all the way to the peaks around Lake O'Hara and Lake Louise. From this high point on the trip, it is a long, continuous descent on gentle slopes to the new and tiny Scott Duncan Hut, which sits on the end of the northwest ridge of Mount Daly (grid reference 416085).

There are several alternative exit routes off the Waputik Icefield, all ending at Wapta Lake. One is to go around the north end of Daly and follow the Bath Glacier. Another, the most common, is to go over the Niles-Daly Col and then descend the chutes above Sherbrooke Lake. Because of the high risk of avalanches in these chutes, a safer route from the col is to contour on a high ledge around the lower south ridge of Mount Niles and then descend through trees and along Sherbrooke Creek.

Both of these latter routes join above Sherbrooke Lake. As you ski across the lake, admire the snow-plastered east face of Mount Ogden. Beyond the lake, a summer trail is followed through trees, traversing left along a sidehill and finally leading to Wapta Lake and the end of the trip.

Cross-Reference Guide

*H*ere is a reference chart that will allow outdoor enthusiasts to determine at a glance what trips or combination of trips they can tackle while in a specific area. Each listing gives a rating, a start to finish distance, an estimated time, and elevation gained from the start to the high point of the trip.

Banff-Lake Louise

Hikes

- Saddleback (p. 29)—Strenuous, 8 kilometres return, 3–4 hours, 580 metres elevation gain.
- Cory Pass Loop (p. 47)—Strenuous, 13 kilometres, 5–7 hours, 900 metres elevation gain.

Backpacks

- Mystic Pass (p. 61)—Strenuous, 37 kilometres, 2 days, 580 metres elevation gain.
- Fish Lakes (p. 58)—Strenuous, 30 kilometres, 2 days, 755 metres elevation gain.

Canoe Trips

- Bow River—Lake Louise to Redearth Creek (p. 89)— Intermediate Open Canadian, 40 kilometres, 5 hours.

Mountain Bike Trips

- Bryant Creek (p. 116)—Intermediate, 40 kilometres, 6 hours, 150 metres elevation gain.

- Mount Rundle Loop (p. 124)—Advanced, 31 kilometres, 5-6 hours, no elevation gain.

Road Cycle Trips

- Jasper to Banff (p. 148)—Strenuous to Advanced, 287 kilometres, 3-5 days, 330 metres elevation gain.
- Bow Valley Parkway (p. 139)—Moderate, 24 kilometres one way, 2-3 hours, slight elevation loss.

Ski Trips

- Sunshine Meadows (p. 169)—Moderate to Intermediate, 20 kilometres, 6-7 hours, 600 metres elevation gain.
- Paradise Valley (p. 171)—Moderate to Intermediate, 20 kilometres, 6 hours, 350 metres elevation gain.
- Skoki Lodge (p. 177)—Intermediate, 25 kilometres, 7 hours, 475 metres elevation gain.
- Healy Pass (p. 181)—Intermediate, 18.5 kilometres, 6-7 hours, 625 metres elevation gain.
- Dolomite Pass (p. 187)—Advanced, 19 kilometres, 6-7 hours, 655 metres elevation gain.
- Wapta Traverse (p. 193)—Advanced—Ski Mountaineering, 50 kilometres, 3-5 days, 1020 metres elevation gain.

Jasper National Park

Hikes

- Cavell Meadows-Angel Glacier Loop (p. 21) —Moderately Strenuous, 8 kilometres, 3-4 hours, 400 metres elevation gain.
- Wilcox Pass (p. 24)—Moderately Strenuous, 8 kilometres, 4 hours, 335 metres elevation gain.
- Sulphur Skyline (p. 35)—Strenuous, 10 kilometres, 3-4 hours, 700 metres elevation gain.

Backpacks

- Brazeau Loop (p. 64)—Strenuous to Advanced, 80 kilometres, 4–5 days, 2100 metres elevation gain.
- Skyline Trail (p. 69)—Advanced, 44 kilometres, 3 days, 820 metres elevation gain.

Canoe Trips

- Athabasca River—Old Fort Point to Highway 16 (p. 91)—Novice Open Canadian, 20 kilometres, 4 hours.

Mountain Bike Trips

- Valley of the Five Lakes to Old Fort Point (p. 121)— Strenuous, 23 kilometres, 3–4 hours, negligible elevation gain.

Road Cycle Trips

- Jasper to Banff (p. 148)—Strenuous to Advanced, 287 kilometres, 3–5 days, 330 metres elevation gain.

Ski Trips

- Moose Lake Loops (p. 162)—Moderate, 8 kilometres, 2 hours, 100 metres elevation gain.
- Bald Hills (p. 174)—Moderate to Intermediate, 11 kilometres, 3–5 hours, 480 metres elevation gain.
- Maccarib Pass (p. 184)—Advanced, 25 kilometres, 7–9 hours, 700 metres elevation gain.

Kananaskis Country

Hikes

- Mount Indefatigable (p. 26)—Strenuous, 7.5 kilometres, 3–4 hours, 500 metres elevation gain.

- Burstall Pass (p. 32)—Strenuous, 15 kilometres, 5–6 hours, 460 metres elevation gain.
- Headwall Lakes (p. 40)—Strenuous, 15 kilometres, 6 hours, 440 metres elevation gain.
- Tyrwhitt Loop (p. 51)—Advanced, 12 kilometres, 6–8 hours, 900 metres elevation gain.

Backpacks

- Aster Lake-Three Isle Lake (p. 73)—Advanced, 41 kilometres, 2–3 days, 1200 metres elevation gain.

Mountain Bike Trips

- Plateau Mountain (p. 111)—Moderate, 12 kilometres, 2–3 hours, 400 metres elevation gain.
- Odlum Pond (p. 114)—Intermediate, 28 kilometres, 4–5 hours, 300 metres elevation gain.
- Moose Mountain (p. 119)—Intermediate, 12 kilometres, 3–4 hours, 470 metres elevation gain.
- Elbow Loop (p. 127)—Advanced, 42 kilometres, 5–8 hours, 640 metres elevation gain.

Road Cycle Trips

- Kananaskis Lakes (p. 136)—Moderate, 29 kilometres, 3–4 hours, minimal elevation gain.
- Highwood Pass (p. 142)—Strenuous, 39 kilometres, 4 hours, 500 metres elevation gain.

Ski Trips

- Elk Pass (p. 165)—Moderate, 12.5 kilometres, 4–5 hours, 245 metres elevation gain.
- Chester Lake (p. 167)—Moderate, 9.5 kilometres, 4 hours, 300 metres elevation gain.
- Robertson-French Loop (p. 190)—Advanced, 20 kilometres, 7–8 hours, 990 metres elevation gain.

Waterton Lakes National Park

Hikes

- Bear's Hump (p. 18)—Moderate, 2.4 kilometres, 1–2 hours, 215 metres elevation gain.
- Rowe Lakes (p. 36)—Strenuous, 13 kilometres, 5–6 hours, 560 metres elevation gain.
- Carthew Summit (p. 42)—Strenuous, 16 kilometres, 6 hours, 660 metres elevation gain.
- Crypt Lake (p. 45)—Strenuous to Advanced, 17 kilometres, 6–7 hours, 670 metres elevation gain.

Calgary Area

Canoe Trips

- Bow River—Bearspaw Dam to Calgary Zoo (p. 89)—Novice Open Canadian, 21 kilometres, 4–5 hours.
- Highwood River—High River to Aldersyde (p. 83)—Novice Open Canadian, 23 kilometres, 4–5 hours.

West-Central Alberta

Canoe Trips

- North Saskatchewan River—Horburg to Brierley Rapids (p. 101)— Intermediate Open Canadian/Novice White Water, 40 kilometres, 5 hours or overnight.

Southeast Alberta

Canoe Trips

- Red Deer River—Dinosaur Provincial Park (p. 86)—Novice Open Canadian, 18 kilometres, 4 hours.

Southern Alberta

Canoe Trips

- Milk River (p. 95)—Novice Open Canadian, 62 kilometres, 2–3 days.

Further Reading

Cycling

Helgason, Gail, and John Dodd. *The Canadian Rockies Bicycling Guide*. Edmonton: Lone Pine Publishing, 1986.

—— *Bicycle Alberta*. Edmonton: Lone Pine Publishing, 1984.

Lepp, Gerhardt. *Backcountry Biking in the Canadian Rockies*. Calgary: Rocky Mountain Books, 1987.

Canoeing

Buhrmann, Hans, and David Young. *Canoeing Chinook Country Rivers*. Lethbridge: 1982.

Canoe Alberta Reach Reports. 4th ed. Edited by Bernice Parry. Edmonton: Travel Alberta, 1978. Six booklets providing details of five major river drainages.

MacDonald, Janice E. *Canoeing Alberta*. Edmonton: Lone Pine Publishing, 1985.

Hiking

Ambrosi, Joey. *Hiking Alberta's Southwest*. Vancouver: Douglas & McIntyre, 1984.

Daffern, Gillean. *Kananaskis Country Trail Guide*. 2d ed. Calgary: Rocky Mountain Books, 1985.

Patton, Brian, and Bart Robinson. *The Canadian Rockies Trail Guide*. 5th ed. Banff: Summerthought, 1992.

Skiing

Daffern, Tony. *Avalanche Safety for Skiers & Climbers.* 2d ed. Calgary: Rocky Mountain Books, 1992.

Scott, Chic. *Ski Trails in the Canadian Rockies.* Calgary: Rocky Mountain Books, 1992.

General

Boles, Glen W., William L. Putnam, and Roger W. Laurilla. *Place Names of the Canadian Alps.* Revelstoke: Footprint Publishing, 1990.

Gadd, Ben. *Handbook of the Canadian Rockies.* Jasper: Corax Press, 1986.

Herrero, Stephen. *Bear Attacks - Their Causes and Avoidance.* New York: Nick Lyon Books, 1985.

Lentz, Martha, Steven Macdonald, and Jan Carline. *Mountaineering First Aid.* 3d ed. Seattle: The Mountaineers, 1985.

Patton, Brian. *Parkways of the Canadian Rockies.* Banff: Summerthought, 1988.

Scotter, George W., and Hälle Flygare. *Wildflowers of the Canadian Rockies.* Edmonton: Hurtig Publishers, 1986.

Scotter, George W., Tom Ulrich, and Edgar T. Jones. *Birds of the Canadian Rockies.* Edmonton: Hurtig Publishers, 1990.

Index

About the Author

*B*ill Corbett is a Calgary writer with interests in the outdoors, the environment, and business. His articles have been published in *Canadian Geographic, Canadian Business, Western Living, Maclean's, Explore,* and other publications. He spends many of his weekends in the Rocky Mountains west of Calgary, climbing, back country skiing, and hiking.